"Brilliantly written and engaging. Cyı̲̲̲̲̲̲̲̲̲̲̲̲̲̲̲̲̲̲̲̲
wisdom make *Anchored* a unique anc
research, combined with biblical and personal stories, creates a ṕ
for guiding the reader through various storms. Cynthia's years of gifted
leadership shine on every page in this exceptional creation."

—Heidi McLaughlin, international speaker and
author of *Restless for More*, *Sand to Pearls*, and *Beauty Unleashed*

"Cynthia Cavanaugh has gifted those in leadership an invaluable resource.
God's call on your life as a leader does not come with a promise for continual
smooth sailing. Through the storms of unanswerable questions, doubts, fears,
and deep wounds, Cynthia anchors you to the scriptural truths that will keep
you steady in the storm."

—Jennifer Kennedy Dean, author of *Live a Praying Life*®,
executive director of The Praying Life Foundation

"No matter what storms we are facing, Cynthia teaches us that if we remain
anchored to Christ, we can weather them all and, most importantly, know we
are never alone."

—Michelle S. Lazurek, award-winning blogger and
author of *Righteous and Lost: Finding Hope for the Pharisee Within*

"In *Anchored*, Cynthia leads us to solid, biblical answers and teaches well the
faith-buoying, redeeming value of a life storm. Perfect for anyone, this book
should have a prime library spot for every Christ follower in any leadership
position. Definitely a read-it-again-and-again resource."

—Rhonda Rhea, TV personality, humor columnist,
author of fourteen books, including *Messy to Meaningful*,
Turtles in the Road, and *Fix Her Upper*

"In *Anchored*, Cynthia Cavanaugh confronts the storms of life with honesty,
courage, and hope. It's a beautiful balance of personal story and insight from
Scripture, reminding us of God's presence and faithfulness. Cynthia gently
challenges us to remember that whatever the storm, no matter how intense
or unrelenting, we can choose to feel safe and protected because of the one
who anchors our souls."

—Jenni Catron, founder of The 4Sight Group and
author of *The Four Dimensions of Extraordinary Leadership*

"Cynthia Cavanaugh's biblically solid approach in *Anchored* addresses the
all too common reality of leaders everywhere in a practical and applicable
way. Every pastor should read this book!"

—Dave Curtiss, vice president of faith engagement,
CRISTA Ministries

"Cynthia Cavanaugh bravely shares her journey of learning to trust God and lead through the storms of life while others are watching. She has done this well, and I encourage you to lean in and learn as I have."

—Helen Burns,
pastor, Relate Church, British Columbia, Canada

"Cynthia Cavanaugh's honesty, authenticity, and biblical insights help us replace our life riggings so we can set sail on God's great adventure for our lives. If you want to avoid shipwreck in your life, pick up this book for yourself and your crew."

—Pam Farrel, codirector of Love-Wise and author and
coauthor of 45 books, including *Discovering Hope in the Psalms:
A Creative Bible Study Experience, 7 Simple Skills for Every Woman:
Success in Keeping Everything Together,* and the best-selling,
Men Are Like Waffles, Women Are Like Spaghetti

"Every leader has faced personal crisis, but not every leader has survived. Cynthia Cavanaugh has not only weathered the storm but has learned the essential secrets of staying anchored even in the storm. Writing authentically, Cynthia invites you into her journey and shows you how to put practices in place to keep you anchored in the crises of life. If you're in any type of leadership role and are longing to leave a godly legacy, this book is a must-read!"

—Becky Harling, international speaker, leadership coach,
and author of *How to Listen So People Will Talk*

"Cynthia has crafted a work that all Christian leaders should keep ready to grab when the inevitable squalls darken our horizon. From storms in her own life, she speaks to the souls of those attempting to lead God's people while battling attacks from without and within. She offers sage counsel gathered from her experiences and from men and women whose stories grace the pages of God's Word."

—Geoffrey Ross Holtz, DD,
senior pastor of The Summit (EFCA), Enumclaw, WA

"*Anchored* is a refreshing book that integrates deep spiritual and leadership principles in the life of a leader and across the divide. When we are refreshed, we have the capacity to do much for those we lead, the collective ministry, and ourselves. As a leader, *Anchored* created change and provided a refreshing perspective on my own spiritual journey."

—Imbenzi George, PhD, Trinity Western University,
Honorary Consul General/Kenyan Diplomat,
executive director, MYERT CORPS INC.

Anchored

Leading Through the Storms

Cynthia
Cavanaugh

NEW HOPE®
PUBLISHERS
Birmingham, Alabama

Other New Hope books by Cynthia Cavanaugh

Unlocked: 5 Myths Holding Your Influence Captive

New Hope® Publishers
5184 Caldwell Mill Rd.
St. 204-221
Hoover, AL 35244
NewHopePublishers.com
New Hope Publishers is a division of Iron Stream Media.

Library of Congress Cataloging-in-Publication Data

Names: Cavanaugh, Cynthia, 1959- author.
Title: Anchored : leading through the storms / Cynthia Cavanaugh.
Description: First [edition]. | Birmingham : New Hope Publishers, 2018.
Identifiers: LCCN 2017050468 | ISBN 9781625915399 (permabind)
Subjects: LCSH: Leadership--Religious aspects--Christianity. |
Storms--Miscellanea. | Bible--Biography.
Classification: LCC BV4597.53.L43 C458 2018 | DDC 253--dc23
LC record available at https://lccn.loc.gov/2017050468

ISBN-13: 978-1-62591-539-9

N184112 • 0218 • 1.5M1

In memory of

Dorothy Lucille Cavanaugh,
my mother-in-law, whose life was marked with joy
and who showed me how to dance in the rain.

ACKNOWLEDGMENTS

When I finished writing the last word of this book, I cried. I felt foolish until my husband said, "You should be crying, you just birthed a baby." It's true; writing a book is like childbirth. You push forward with everything you can mentally, emotionally, spiritually, and yes, even physically. (Especially when you are stiff from sitting in one place too long). Writing becomes the obsession as deadlines approach. Along the way, you gather friends and family who become your cheerleaders as you round the last lap.

Thank you, New Hope Publishers, for continuing to believe in me as a writer. The team is a blessing, and I am grateful.

To all those who gave me permission to tell a small piece of your story so that others could be inspired, Heather DeVries, Vicki Doubroff, Koby and Jenna Liesch, and Heidi McLaughlin.

To my sister Heidi who continues to hold me accountable, prays for me, and believes in me when I don't believe in myself. To my Aunt Trudy who reminds me my writing is a gift and God will give me what I need to finish the project. To my mom and dad, who pray for me, and my dad in particular, who makes me feel like a *New York Times* bestselling author.

To my best cheerleader in life and friendship, Cheryl. To my AWSA sisters (Advanced Writers and Speakers Association), my MasterMind and Diva Prayer Girls and writing tribe, thank you for mentoring me along the journey.

To my students and staff at Trinity Western University who sharpen me as a leader and give me the honor to teach and lead.

To my sons, Jeremy, Jordan, and Jason, and their wives, Emily, Julie, and Brittany, for being an incredible support. For your encouragement to pursue my calling and understanding when I had to reluctantly say no to doing what I delight in the most—nurturing and spending time with my grandchildren.

To my husband Kevin, my friend and companion who sat and listened to every word of this book as each chapter was complete and gave helpful feedback. He made meals and gave me the courage to finish when I felt pressed to meet the deadline.

Lastly, to Jesus Christ, the lover of my soul, who gets all the credit for the words contained in these pages. He sustains me and gives life in the storms and leads me to flourish even when life gets hard. He is my comfort, my joy, and my song.

Contents

Introduction ix

Chapter One
  The Perfect Storm
  Jesus and the Disciples: Facing Fear 1

Chapter Two
  Hurricane Hopelessness
  Job: Unpredictable Catastrophes 13

Chapter Three
  Tornadoes and Twisted Truth
  Eli and Sons: Leading Your Family 25

Chapter Four
  Firestorm Fallout
  Paul and Barnabas: Sharp Disagreements 37

Chapter Five
  Ice Storms, Icy Souls
  Esau: Respecting Your Birthright 49

Chapter Six
  Lightning Learning
  Timothy: Intentional Learning 63

Chapter Seven
   Tropical Storm Testing
   Tabitha: Resurrecting Dead Dreams............................75

Chapter Eight
   Derecho Devastation
   Nehemiah: Rebuilding Broken Teams........................85

Chapter Nine
   Haboob Havoc
   David: When You Doubt...99

Chapter Ten
   Cyclones of Uncertainty
   Priscilla and Aquila: Trusting in the Unknown.........107

Chapter Eleven
   Flood Faith
   Levites and Priests: Leading in Faith........................115

Chapter Twelve
   Snowstorm Temptations
   Moses: Learning to Delegate 127

Chapter Thirteen
   Worry Winds
   Elijah: The Pitfall of Fatigue....................................135

Chapter Fourteen
   Tempest Trials
   Judas and Jesus: Betrayal 143

Chapter Fifteen
   The Gathering Storm
   King Jehoshaphat: Leading into the Future.............155

Introduction

When they walk through the Valley of Weeping,
it will become a place of refreshing springs. The
autumn rains will clothe it with blessings.

—Psalm 84:6 NLT

I like rain puddles. I like jumping and splashing in them,
mud and all. When I was a teenager, I had to walk about
a quarter of a mile home down a winding road from the
bus stop. On rainy days, my favorite thing to do was dance
in the puddles when no one was looking. I grew up in the
Pacific Northwest, and rain is simply part of our DNA. As
a Washington resident, puddle jumping is nearly a sport,
as with most kids who live in this section of the country.

In the northwest corner of the United States, we affec-
tionately refer to ourselves as having webbed feet. The
average rainfall around the city I live in is 35.8 inches
annually with 163 days of rain a year. That's a lot of rain!
I might add there is no prettier place on earth on a bright
sunny day. In addition to the rain, myriad storms move
in and out of our region. Living with the mountains on
one side and the Pacific Ocean on the other makes for
some brilliant storms. In a period of just a few hours, we
can have snow, hail, sleet, sunshine, lightning, torrential
rains, and thunderstorms. In our homes, we have what we
call coat closets because we need a whole closet of boots,
coats, and umbrellas just to be prepared for whatever
storm may descend on any given day. Being tough and
willing to weather the storms is part of navigating life in
the Pacific Northwest, as is making sure the storms don't

submerge us. This is true whether the storms require a coat or a lot of prayer.

After all, life can be a series of storms, and I wish it were as easy as going to my coat closet to pick out the right coat for the right weather. Storms in life can be complicated. Sometimes they are confusing and devastating. Other times they are more like those small funnel clouds you might see at the side of the road in a dry climate. They swirl and stir up dust but don't cause much damage. Even still they are unsettling. Jesus talked about storms and gave us instruction on how to not just survive a storm but how to weather it bravely.

Mark 4 tells the story of the storm we are probably most familiar with in the Bible. The disciples were out on the Sea of Galilee with Jesus when a furious storm arose and the boat began to fill with water. And while the disciples panicked, Jesus slept. Full of desperation, they woke Him. And if you read the rest of the story, you know He calmed the storm. But here is the kicker; Jesus rebuked the disciples and asked them, "Why are you so afraid? Have you still no faith?" (v. 40). It seems a ridiculous question, but Jesus asks them for a reason. He wants to make sure we get the point of being in a storm. Front and center in the story, if not most stories in our lives, lay the answer—*trust Jesus.* At the risk of sounding too simplistic, there are treasures hidden in that little word *trust.* Trust calls us to action. When in a storm, Jesus calls us to ante up and choose to find our faith and make a choice to boldly hold on tight.

I can't fault the disciples for their lack of faith. I know I would be going crazy if I saw my boat filling with water as the winds tossed me around. The central point in this story is that the disciples weren't alone; Jesus was with them not only in the boat but also in the heart of the storm. This book is about just that: finding your faith and learning to stand strong in your personal storm.

If you serve in any capacity of leadership, you know how critical it is to remain anchored in the storm. Why? Because people are watching! It's not just about you or me when we are caught up in the waves of a storm. Those who follow us and are influenced by us carefully observe our response in crisis. If you are a pastor or church leader, your team *and* others in the church watch the choices you make while navigating a storm. If you are a leader and influencer in your community, people are watching your steps and observing your character. If you are a parent, grandparent, aunt, uncle, cousin, sister, or brother, your family is cluing into how you will keep integrity in the midst of the storm.

When reading this classic story, God downloaded a fresh perspective for me.

> Late that day he said to them, Let's go across to the other side. They took him in the boat as he was. Other boats came along.
>
> —Mark 4:35–36 *The Message*

Did you catch the last sentence? Other boats came along. I've read this story probably hundreds of times and never noticed the last sentence. I believe it's paramount to the story and is a visual for us as leaders. The disciples were in the boat with Jesus. And they might not have realized it, but they were influencers. The people in the other boats were watching the disciples' response to not only the storm but to Jesus. They might have been thinking, *If the disciples can trust Jesus in this storm, then I can trust Him too!*

You may not be in a storm just yet, or maybe you are full on in a horrific superstorm. Wherever you find yourself, know your faith and God's grace will not let you sink and drown. This assurance is one we understand in our heads, but when a storm converges it can trigger a memory loss of the faithfulness of God. We can just plain forget. The pain can override our faith. Let me say this boldly: You are not alone in the boat in your storm. Jesus is in the boat, in the storm, and in the circumstances, and He is the only one who can deliver peace. I believe you will come through with increased endurance able to confidently flourish as you activate your faith. It is a choice, and you can rest in the boat because you know Jesus is there and He is worthy of your trust. Those who are watching from the other boats will see faith in action and be encouraged.

Get your rain boots ready. You will be able to dance in the puddles after the rain.

Chapter One
THE PERFECT STORM

Jesus and the Disciples: Facing Fear

> I am not afraid of storms for I am learning how to sail my ship.
>
> —Louisa May Alcott

On September 20, 1991, six fishermen in Gloucester, Massachusetts, kissed their families and said goodbye to board the 72-foot steel-hulled swordfish vessel, the *Andrea Gail*. Toward the end of the fishing venture in late October, they encountered a storm of unprecedented strength. While it was officially called the "the Halloween nor'easter of 1991," many people now remember it as "the perfect storm" because of Sebastian Junger's book and the movie that followed.

This nor'easter came from the merger of three separate storms. Vessels reported waves the equivalent of ten-story buildings. And the *Andrea Gail* crew found themselves trapped right in the middle of it. On October 28, the *Andrea Gail*, now surrounded by massive waves and increasing winds, made one final radio transmission describing the conditions they were sustaining. The captain gave their position and signed off. There was no further contact.

Rescue and search teams found a few of the boat's fuel drums, along with other items from the wreckage, but found no trace of its six men. The crew was declared lost. The community of Gloucester was devastated.

Like the merging conditions that caused the perfect storm in 1991, life can create a perfect storm. With no warning, we can find ourselves heading right toward the eye of a deadly storm. We can lose perspective, meander over our thoughts, and ask the question, why? It can feel as though a ten-story wave will submerge us and leave us hopeless and unable to recover.

My perfect storm began in 2007. Life was good. I was living the dream for Jesus. My family and ministry were flourishing. God had blown the doors wide open for ministry opportunities. I stood in awe as invitations to speak and write flooded in. In truth, I was partly scared out of my mind. But I felt God's delight as I taught His Word, encouraging women to live life boldly with godly influence. I was telling my God story and watching Him draw women to Himself in incredible ways. I was overwhelmed and incredibly humbled as I listened faithfully to God's whispering, "You can do this, I have given you everything you need to succeed." I wanted to be obedient to use the gifts He had entrusted to me.

But by the end of 2007, I was utterly exhausted from years of ministry, traveling, and the major family events that marched on in spite of my busy schedule. Our last big family event came when our middle son was married after a whirlwind romance. My husband Kevin and I were on the verge of an empty nest. I needed rest . . . and more. Since I had experienced clinical depression in the past, I knew the warning signs and what I needed to do to restore.

At the same time, Kevin's influence as a pastor and leader was growing. God had us on parallel tracks, and soon we were both running in separate directions on a national level like two bullet trains. At first, we had a blast. We had our God story-time catch up moments, engaging conversations, and times of prayer together. After a while, it became apparent something was amiss. Just as in the perfect storm of 1991, our storm had three distinct pieces that came together, lurking to erupt into something we couldn't even imagine.

The first storm came as one by one our boys left the nest. Admittedly, I had never understood the empty nest woes. In fact, when I heard women wailing about their kids growing up and moving out, I used to think, *What is wrong with them?* I never imagined I would be sad about it *at all*. Here I stood at the edge of the nest, ready to turn in my mother badge after 28 years. Of course, I was silly, or so I thought. I knew I would always be a mother, right? A significant shift was on its way, and my emotions were completely unprepared. I found myself mentally moping around. I felt like the father in the movie *My Big Fat Greek Wedding* when his daughter is about to get married, and he laments over and over, "Why you want to leave me?" Of course, my little chicks were now grown men with chest hair, and it was time to cut the ties. They were flourishing, and I was so very proud of them, but it was an emotional nightmare to close that chapter in my life. It took me by surprise. I tried to communicate the best I could to my husband, but he kept declaring, "We are free, we are free, thank God, we are free at last!" That didn't help much, as you can imagine.

The second storm brewing out in our little ocean was our growing ministry. Kevin and I became two ships passing in the night. As much as we tried to manage everything, we weren't as healthy in our marriage as we thought. We believed we were doing the right things—going on dates every week, taking vacations and weekends away—but deep down the core of our marriage foundation had a crack that weakened our ability to connect and relate. But we mustered on in Jesus' name, of course. God's kingdom needed us! We just didn't have time to pay attention to the crack that kept widening, unaware it was becoming a serious chasm.

The last significant storm was an inner nagging something was wrong. And when I say wrong, I mean, *awful*. Our marriage needed repairs like an old familiar house that begins showing wear and tear. We'd had years of unacknowledged dysfunction, even though we believed we were doing all the right things to keep our marriage thriving. However, it wasn't enough to ward off the slow-growing cancer that eventually turned into an all-out metastatic infection.

The pressure in our lives intensified as we continued the cycle of conflicted reactions. Wrong belief systems of what a healthy marriage should look like and unhealthy patterns kept bubbling to the surface and oozing out danger. We stepped around it, ignored the warning signs, and tried to adhere bandages when what we really needed was serious surgery. But we were too busy to check into the hospital. As the pressure mounted for both of us, our unhealthy cycles increased in frequency—from once a year to every three months to every few weeks to nearly every few days. We had lost the ability to reason with one another, and our home became a hotbed of fighting.

It wrecked both of us. It was emotionally and physically exhausting. My husband turned into someone I didn't recognize. He was angry, and my reactive emotional behavior in return was frightening. I thought I was losing my mind.

We tried attending counseling together—two different counselors—and that just made it worse. We each needed individual counseling before we could reap the benefits of sitting in counseling sessions together. We stopped going as a couple, and I continued to go myself.

As my husband buried himself in his ministry and work, I withdrew. We stayed in our separate corners, smiling in public as our marriage crumbled behind closed doors.

After about a year of counseling, God revealed my severe codependency. I learned this meant I felt responsible for making everyone happy at any cost, even to myself. I wasn't being honest with what I was feeling or thinking, and that fed the dysfunction in our marriage. Of course, being the good Christian girl, I tried so hard to do everything right. When my world fell apart, I was dumbfounded. It was then I came to the pinnacle of the crisis.

I made a hard choice, and for my emotional well-being, I felt led to take a time-out. I made the decision to separate for a short period of time and move out of our home. It wasn't an easy decision and a very unconventional one for the wife of a pastor. I agonized and prayed. Then prayed some more. I sought counsel for months on end because I desperately wanted to do the right thing. The last thing I wanted was to hurt anyone, but I knew if I continued in this way, eventually there would be severe ramifications emotionally and physically. I was losing myself, and the noise of the fierce wind and waves overwhelmed my heart.

I knew the possible consequences of what was at stake. My husband could lose his job if I made the decision to separate. When your husband is the pastor, your marriage and your family are seen as the models to follow. Not in the perfect sense but in the sense that a pastor is called to be the shepherd of the church. If his home is out of order, how can he be expected to lead effectively? Most churches wouldn't look favorably at a pastor whose marriage was falling apart. At the very least a sabbatical or professional help would need to be offered.

So I knew we could lose everything—not only his job but also the ministry God had entrusted to us up to that point. But with the support of my counselor and a few leaders, I took a time-out and moved out for three months. I wish I could tell you everything was fixed in those three months and that the storm subsided, but it didn't. The winds howled louder, and the waves crashed around the struggle of our crisis.

The one different thing was that I chose to hold onto only Jesus in the boat with all of my might, white knuckles and all.

Up until that point, I had made my incredible leader-pastor husband an idol. I had elevated him to a place only God should be, and it was a sin. God is very clear in the Bible about putting other gods before Him. My dysfunction and trying to make everyone happy at whatever cost caused my heart to shut down. I didn't fully understand Proverbs 4:23, where we are instructed to, "Keep your heart with all vigilance, for from it flow the springs of life." I was beginning to get a glimpse of what it meant to keep my heart through Psalm 71: "For you, O Lord, are my hope, my trust, O Lord, from my youth" (v. 5). He gently rebuked me and helped me revisit the spiritual marker of my relationship with Jesus before I met Kevin. God reminded me that He was to be the sole voice of authority, my hope, and my confidence. My husband was important, but he was broken like myself, and together we needed to seek Jesus' restoration.

The storm grew considerably darker as a result of the decision to separate. I lost friends. There were betrayals, rebukes, and spiritual abuse—all initiated by people I believed cared about me. My greatest fear—being misunderstood—had come to pass, and this reached the epitome of misunderstanding on so many levels. The hardest part was knowing I would disappoint our kids. And even though they were adults and had left home, I felt like a complete failure. I rocked their world, especially our youngest son and his wife. I moved out shortly after they were married, and the timing was not ideal; it crushed them. Each of our sons handled it in the best way they could, but it was tough, and it hurt. I am so proud of each of them, and they didn't take sides; they prayed. In turn, in the process, I wanted—even in my pain the best way I knew how—to honor their dad even though we were both bleeding inside. I felt pain like I had never experienced before, but in the midst of it all, God's love poured over my broken heart. I had to choose to believe that God was near even though the painful wounds raged screaming otherwise.

Our church didn't shun us or remove Kevin as pastor. Instead, they loved us through the mess, sent us to counseling and two separate gut-wrenching weeklong intensives in the mountains of Colorado and city of Dallas. The Master Physician Jesus, through skillful surgeons led by the Holy Spirit, lanced the cancer in our marriage. He didn't fix it all immediately, but the Holy Spirit exposed the dysfunction, peeling back the layers so we could see the next steps we needed in order to take to get well.

The winds and waves have calmed considerably during the time of awareness and healing. We have watched God breathe renewed life into our marriage and repair unhealthy patterns and a belief system so deeply entrenched in the corridors of our minds. We've set boundaries and limits so we don't end up repeating the same storm pattern again. Are we perfect? Not by a long shot, but we are growing and having fun together again. We came very close to ending our marriage for good. I know not every story has an ending like ours. We aren't living happily ever after, but rather we are healing, growing, and learning to love each other in new ways. Most importantly, we are learning how to forgive.

When I began sharing my story at leadership conferences and women's retreats, I realized I was not alone.

Isn't it ironic how the enemy uses this weapon skillfully to isolate us from each other when we need community the most? Many marriages and specifically leadership marriages encounter similar types of storms, even a perfect storm like ours.

This kind of storm weighs heavily on my heart because I know that as our world gets darker, ministry leadership gets more complicated. How do we as leaders and influencers weather the unexpected and sometimes not-so-unexpected storms that come to us? What do we do? Do we leave our positions? Do we stop doing God's work? How do we handle those we lead? Who do we tell? Where do we run for godly counsel and help? These are some of the many questions I hope to address in the following pages as we talk about storms in general. I don't pretend to know the answers, but I do know the God who has the right answer for each person and situation. There is certainly not a one-size-fits-all formula.

In the murkiest part of the storm, I found that Jesus was always in my boat on the roughest waves, and it fed my hope. I believe hope isn't a feeling but is embodied in the person of Jesus Christ, and He promises to journey with you and me. I want to unpack this truth further as we revisit the story when the disciples were in the boat with Jesus and the great storm rose on the sea.

> Then he got in the boat, his disciples with him. The next thing they knew, they were in a severe storm. Waves were crashing into the boat—and he was sound asleep! They roused him, pleading, "Master, save us! We're going down!" Jesus reprimanded them. "Why are you such cowards, such faint-hearts?" Then he stood up and told the wind to be silent, the sea to quiet down: "Silence!" The sea became smooth as glass.
>
> —Matthew 8:23–26 *The Message*

I wonder how many of you feel like the disciples—watching the waves mounting to a perfect storm and thinking Jesus is oblivious to your situation. And you aren't able to quite see that God has the storm under control because your perspective is clouded. Or maybe you aren't sure if your radio contact with God is being received and heard. Doubt creeps in, and fear and anxiety run amok in your mind along with discouragement and depression. These are all signs of a perfect storm seeking to converge and lure us away from our loving God and Savior.

We have a very real enemy who wants to defeat us and take us out on all levels, in the test, in the trial. Satan, the enemy of our soul, wants us to get lost in the storm, get off course, distrust God, and be fearful of the future. His plan is for us to quit. I've been there! And if he can get those three things to line up and collide with each other, then he has won. It's about winning for him, and we can't let him win. We have the resurrection power to defeat him right in the storm when he whispers lies to discourage us. He wants us to forget the battle was already won on the Cross. There is too much at stake to opt out of taking our position in Christ because we are miserable in the storm. Victory is promised!

So here are a few things I've observed as I have learned from my perfect storm in this story.

1. Jesus got in the boat, and the disciples followed Him.

    When we choose to follow Jesus as the disciples did, God holds the pen, and He owns the rights to our story. He does the writing of my life and your life as we submit to Him. Our stories start when we are born. Each event becomes a chapter in an exclusive story of how God draws us to Himself. When you and I choose to follow Him, we walk together with different circumstances like each of the disciples as they decided to follow Him.

This concept hit me like bricks when I was at a simulcast conference and the speaker, Priscilla Shirer, talked about Gideon and how God had given Gideon everything he needed up to that point to do what God was asking him to do. As I sat there, I felt as though God rushed into a devastated piece of my soul and whispered, "I have prepared you and your whole life for this very moment of this storm. I will give you exactly what you need to not only survive but to thrive. Can you trust Me?" I sat and cried, oblivious to the other women around me.

2. Our storms don't take God by surprise—ever, ever. He is the God of even the fiercest, unexpected events in our lives.

Notice what Scripture says, "Suddenly a furious storm came up on the lake, so that the waves swept over the boat" (Matthew 8:24 NIV).

It was unannounced; it came up suddenly when the sky was entirely clear. Let me explain how this happens on the Sea of Galilee.

To understand the causes of these sudden and violent tempests, we must remember that the Galilee lies low—680 feet below sea level. It is thirteen miles long and nearly eight miles wide, and the squalls come down from the Golan Heights with terrific force. The original Greek words used to describe the storm are *seismos megas*, like an earthquake. So it is no exaggeration it was a violent, furious tempest that came up suddenly.

3. The storm came in the midst of the disciple's obedience to Jesus.

I am still reflecting on this truth, and it is changing the way I think about the storms that come in my life. Remember, the disciples followed Jesus willingly into the boat. They had no idea what was about to happen. It wasn't a storm like what happened to Jonah. He disobeyed God and ran away, and then God sent a storm to motivate him to obedience.

When you and I follow Jesus, we will encounter storms unexpectedly, and we shouldn't be surprised! God leads us to follow Him into a storm not to destroy us but to develop us. Wrap your brain around that one!

Storms happen. Our human nature wants to lead us to the exact opposite. It's difficult to comprehend the expression of unconditional love within a human framework. Or to think God might lead us to something that could hurt us or will be a part of a better future plan.

We might be tempted to think . . .

What have I done to cause this storm?

What have I done wrong?

I know my brain has gone down that path many more times than I can count.

I am learning that God's love over us isn't conditional. The disciples hadn't done anything wrong; they just followed Jesus into the boat voluntarily like baby ducks following their momma across a lake.

And that's what we do when we follow Jesus and give our lives to Him. We follow Him right into the boat and sometimes unknowingly right into a storm. He doesn't leave us alone. He is with us. We may think He is sleeping or not paying attention, but He is riding the storm out with us and promises never to leave us—ever!

So hunker down in the bottom of the boat and know that Jesus isn't far. He is very present. It might feel like He is sleeping, but He is right there watching the weather and how it impacts you and me. He counts the rhythmic force of the waves and gives us exactly what we need not just to make it through but to have peace.

Take a minute to write down the part of the story in which you find yourself.

What do you know about Jesus that can help give you assurance in your storm?

What do you know to be true of His character?

Post a list where you can see it daily to remind you of His presence in your boat.

Chapter Two

HURRICANE HOPELESSNESS

Job: Unpredictable Catastrophes

> We must accept finite disappointment but never lose infinite hope.
>
> —Martin Luther King Jr.

He was devastated. Courier after courier came. Messenger after messenger arrived and delivered the news. All was lost. All was gone. The greatest and wealthiest of all people of the East lost everything, including his beloved children. Job's story is one of those in the Bible that causes you to stop and take a second look. He was blameless, full of integrity and character, and yet God allowed a storm, a hurricane, to sweep across Job's personal landscape and cause devastation beyond human understanding. God gave Satan permission to test Job, and from the beginning, it was said of him, "In all this Job did not sin or charge God with wrong" (Job 1:22). In other words, he didn't blame God. Job encountered what we might call a hurricane bent on leading him to a place of hopelessness.

Hurricanes are some of the most destructive storms on the earth. Rainfall, accompanied by wind, can cause widespread flooding and destruction. One only has to remember the devastation in Houston, Texas, from Hurricane Harvey, which killed more than fifty people and displaced more than one million. It damaged 200,000 homes and left a wide swath of devastation covering 300 miles. It has been recorded as the most deadly and costly hurricane, surpassing Hurricanes Katrina or Sandy, toppling nearly $180 billion.

Texas is no stranger to deadly storms. One of the deadliest hurricanes on US soil was in 1900 on the upper Texas coast. Between 8,000 and 12,000 lives were lost, 3,000 homes destroyed, and about $30 million worth of damage was caused.

Unlike tornadoes, which rarely last more than a few hours, hurricanes can last for days and weeks. Beyond the horrific winds, the storm surge causes rainfall that increases flooding and poses the greatest threat for destruction.

You might say Job experienced in the first round the winds of complete havoc of losing everything he owned and, most precious of all, his children. If you want the full account, read Job 1:13–19. As if that wasn't horrific enough, the second wave came in the long and drawn out rainfall and flooding of his personal health and emotional well-being found in Job 2:7–8 where he was afflicted with oozing sores from head to toe. Both times following these hurricane-like encounters, Job keeps his integrity. Even when his wife challenges him saying, "Do you still hold fast your integrity? Curse God and die" (v. 9), Job responds, "You speak as one of the foolish women would speak. Shall we receive good from God, and shall we not receive evil? In all this Job did not sin with his lips" (v. 10).

We don't know the agony in his mind at the time, but Job kept his integrity. He held fast and stayed silent lest he compromise his integrity at that moment. Job was a man of influence, honor, and authority. He was a leader of leaders, and even when he was tested he was steadfast in his integrity.

Job was like us. He suffered. He wept. He reflected. He questioned. Facing God's silence and the not-so-comforting comments by well-meaning friends, he drops into what St. John of the Cross calls the "dark night of the soul." St. John was a Carmelite monk who helped to reform the Carmelite Order and endured great suffering and even prison for his efforts. His writings have become part of the classics of Christian literature for his intimacy with God and his desire to help others. St. John says, "The endurance of darkness, is the preparation for great light." It appears Job finds himself enduring great darkness, and yet God seems silent and absent for a long while.

In the places of fierce testing, what do we hold onto? What anchors us? How do we keep from sliding off the cliff into the abyss of no return and, as Job's wife wanted him to, curse God and die?

Our anchor points come from what takes place before the storm hits and not necessarily during or after. After Hurricane Katrina in 2005, there were speculations that design flaws were the reason the levees failed in the City of New Orleans, increasing the devastation. Others say it wouldn't have mattered how secure the levees were, Katrina was just too catastrophic of a storm. Whichever it was, the truth is, what we build into our lives before the storm becomes the anchor points in which we hold onto when our world is shaken by a hurricane. When the wind and waves threaten to submerge us permanently, the anchor points keep us moored steadfast in Jesus.

FEMA has a document on its website on how to prepare for a hurricane. It provides clear instructions on how to minimize damage by planning ahead for evacuation, communication, prepping your home, and storing supplies. They don't guarantee you will emerge from the hurricane unscathed, but these preparatory steps help individuals sustain a storm. Wisdom says that if you live in a hurricane region, it is wise to know ahead of time so it doesn't totally take you by surprise.

Job isn't taken by surprise; he knew he wasn't exempt from pain and suffering. Although his hurricane didn't give him any warning, he still was in the "know" and had anchor points to sustain him through the storm. He had been practicing for years and lived a life that kept him tethered to God. The anchors are what carried him through the shouting whispers of doubt that God had abandoned him and the diatribes from his well-meaning friends trying to help him figure God out.

Practice and Fearing God

Job built three anchors into his life that we find in the first chapter. These kept him positioned to weather the most titanic storm he ever encountered.

The first anchor is found in Job 1:1, "There was a man in the land of Uz whose name was Job, and that man was blameless and upright, one who feared God and turned away from evil." Plain and straightforward, Job had laid the greatest anchor—fearing God and remaining blameless and upright for the preparation of the storm ahead. The NIV translation says he "shunned evil." That meant he feared God in every area of his life possible, which kept him from the temptation of giving way to evil actions and behaviors. Was he perfect? No, of course not. But even God himself said this of Job to Satan when he appeared before God and was looking to stir up trouble: "Have you considered my servant Job, that there is none like him on the earth, a blameless and upright man, who fears God and turns away from evil?" (Job 2:3).

Job built into his life the characteristics of fearing God. Blameless and upright is a tall order, but Job was no different from you or me. We might be tempted to think

Job didn't struggle. We would be foolish to believe he somehow had an ethereal connection toward perfect behavior and was immune from temptation. He was tempted to give in to the vices of his day; they just looked different.

God commends him for making a choice to turn away, a choice only made possible by Job's decision to anchor himself to God. He turned away and shunned the evil that paraded by him. It is true for us as well. The root is the same; anything that would take us away from God keeps us in the running to embrace evil.

To shun evil means we have to daily embrace Jesus knowing that we need Him every moment of every hour. We must turn away from our sinful ways and abandon the temptations continually placed in front of us. It isn't a cake walk, but I want to remind us of our anchor. God makes it possible through His Son Jesus Christ, and we don't have to do anything in our strength. How often have we heard this, known this, tried this, taught this, but didn't access the power to push back the sin in our life through Jesus Christ? We give up, give in, beat ourselves up, and believe it isn't a reality. I would counter otherwise. It is possible to live like Job—fearing God, blameless, upright, and turning away from evil. It is a daily choice we make against raging emotions that tell us otherwise. When we stand in the power of Jesus, we live in the same category as Job. We learn to fear God. It isn't a one-time declaration. It is a moment-by-moment choice learning to trust God through each circumstance.

Never did I understand the magnitude of what it means to fear God and make godly decisions than when it was spelled out to me plain and simple about an anger problem I had as a young wife and mom. There were times I would become so impatient my frustrations would erupt hot lava and ash on anyone unfortunate enough to be nearby.

Mainly this happened behind closed doors in my home with my husband and children, and it was ugly. Giving in and uncapping the frustration onto my family immediately felt exhilarating, but seeing the hurt and pain registered on their faces quickly caused me to despair.

I can remember a good friend pointing out to me that when I let the volcano loose, I was making a choice to cross the line. In turn, I was choosing at that moment to rebel against God by not fearing Him in my life. Ouch! That was a harsh statement, and yet it was the truth I needed to hear. I had never framed my eruptions like that before. I desperately wanted to please God, and yet I was doing the very thing I didn't want to do as Paul said in Romans 7:15, "For I do not understand my own actions. For I do not do what I want, but I do the very thing I hate." I soon learned that with Christ's strength I could make the right choice to fear God in my frustration and take steps to control my anger. Fearing God is the anchor that kept Job stable in the hurricane, and it is the anchor that keeps us as well. It is our FEMA document for hurricane preparedness.

The Responsibility of Our Legacy

Another of Job's anchors is his recognition of the responsibility of his legacy to his children. His kids would party and feast together, and "When the parties were over, Job would get up early in the morning and sacrifice a burnt offering for each of his children, thinking, 'Maybe one of them sinned by defying God inwardly'" (Job 1:5 *The Message*). Job made a habit of this sacrificial atonement, just in case they'd sinned.

Job bore the weight of responsibility for his children of passing on a godly legacy. He made a conscious decision. He not only feared God and shunned evil, but he took his parenting seriously. Our legacy matters! We choose our

legacy. If we don't choose a godly heritage, the le
be determined for us. Sadly, we will reflect thing
not want to be remembered for.

Job was intentional. He cared about the spiritual
well-being of his children and practiced the Old Testament rituals of atonement for sin. Today we don't have to
practice the same rituals Job did, and yet we too are called
to care for the spiritual well-being of those around us. As
leaders and influencers, this is of particular importance for
our families. They are the ones who will glean the most
from our legacy. We may have hundreds and thousands of
followers as leaders, but our most intimate relationships
are the people who are impacted the greatest.

My husband and I have lived in public ministry for
nearly four decades. I have come to realize that I am more
concerned about how my children—and now my grandchildren—see me than I am about how any others in
ministry see me. My closest relationships are the ones I
need to be intentional about choosing the characteristics
of my legacy.

Job modeled godliness to his children, and he also carried the spiritual banner for his family. What should that
look like for us? It means we intentionally, or "continually" as the Job passage declares in the NIV translation,
pray for our children and our children's children. I am the
product of praying grandparents. I know I am who I am
today because of my grandparents' prayers. They took
their legacy seriously. And today, my parents do the same.
My mom keeps a prayer journal and prays daily for us.
Those prayers cover my soul like a warm blanket, and
knowing prayer is spoken over me helps me remember
I am not alone.

My dad recently said his favorite time of the day was
getting up early and sitting in his chair by the window. He
told me he reads his Bible and talks to God about all the

things in his heart. He prays for me, my two sisters, our families, and all his grandchildren and great-grandchildren. He is choosing the same legacy as Job. He not only cares about his family, but he cares about our spiritual well-being enough to day in and day out intercede on our behalf. I can't tell you as a daughter what it means to know my dad prays for me every single day. This wasn't always a part of his routine, and yet as my dad has aged he has chosen to set this example for us, and it gives me great comfort to know I am sheltered in my daddy's prayers.

Fearing God and practicing the responsibility of the legacy are two important anchors that held Job when the hurricane winds threatened to destroy him.

Worship Even When the Wind and Waves Reach Higher

The wind whipped poor Job around for months. He had no relief for a long, long time. But he did something rather phenomenal. He worshipped. And he didn't start worshipping when the winds blew; he'd had practice and plenty of it. This is the third anchor Job built into his life.

Job often practiced worshipping God as he sought to carry the torch of his family's legacy. Because he continually made a habit of consecrating his family in presenting them to God, it isn't a surprise that we find him worshipping God soon after he received the news of losing his family. The family he prayed for continually. The children he carried the torch for, the children he loved and cared for with all of his heart. Yet in his grief he worshipped. "Then Job arose and tore his robe and shaved his head and fell on the ground and worshiped. And he said, 'Naked I came from my mother's womb, and naked shall I return. . . .' In all this Job did not sin or charge God with wrong" (Job 1:20–22).

What I find incredibly admirable about Job in this instance is there is no way I believe Job could have worshipped at this point if he had not regularly been practicing worship in his life when all was well. His devotion put him in a position to receive the good and the bad because he knew who was at the center of his soul. It was God and not himself. He was thrust deep into the pit of pain, and yet He still could worship. How can we understand this? I am not entirely sure, but I do know of others who have experienced this same phenomenon, and I believe it is because God already has an anchor in their souls.

Weeks before Christmas, my dear friend Heidi had to say goodbye to her husband. She and her "darling Jack," as she called him, had been married twenty years and were just about to take a trip to New York to celebrate their anniversary when he had a massive heart attack and died. But somehow, as I've watched her in her grief these past several months, she has been a rock. Not because she is devoid of emotion but because she is like Job—anchored in Jesus. Even more, this isn't the first time Heidi has dealt with the death of a husband. She lost her first husband around the same time of year; he also died of a heart attack. She buried two husbands in twenty-four years. I can hardly wrap my brain around the kind of pain she is experiencing. Even though her pain is deep and wide, her faith is more profound. I believe with every promise from God's Word that she will get through this. Not because she is a super-saint, but because she knows who is at the center of her soul. She has permanently etched God's truth over her heart and life. She practices. She prepares. Even though she had no clue what was coming. She worships even now. I marvel when I hear the words of truth and worship that pour forth from her mouth. She knows that "He who calls you is faithful; he will surely do it" (1 Thessalonians 5:24).

I wouldn't wish a hurricane like Heidi's on anyone. We are not immune to devastation and suffering in our lives.

Hope can be found because hope is found in a person, Jesus Christ. The anchors keep us grounded.

When our world is turned upside down, if we haven't practiced these truths while right-side up, what makes you or I think we will be able to withstand the onslaught during the storm and keep our integrity like Job? The choices we make ahead of time determine the choices we will make during the storm. And I am not talking about the possibility of falling into a brief heap of despair or taking a few steps sideways to make ourselves feel better like going on a shopping or eating binge. The biggest temptation we will ever face in a storm is whether or not we believe God has abandoned, forgotten, and rejected us when the hurricane winds rip through and the floodwaters rise.

In the midst of my perfect storm after Kevin and I separated, I was settling into my little apartment all by myself, and I remember thinking I could either make a choice right there to believe that God was God, or I could walk away from every truth about Jesus I had ever known since my childhood. Was He there in my darkness? Would my heart ever be whole again? Could I trust God when I felt rejected and betrayed by others? Could I believe every promise in the Bible? These are the questions I turned over and over in my mind.

I was forced to make a choice—to take a step of faith into the unknown or fall into the temptation of relying on my wisdom and believing God had abandoned me. That's how much the core of my soul ached. I made an intentional decision that no matter what was ahead—with all the what-ifs—I would fear God and trust Him even though I couldn't see the bigger picture. It certainly looked bleak at the time. It wasn't the natural choice; it was the hardest decision I've ever made to continue to trust God and believe Him. As I look back, I am grateful for the months and years of securing the anchor ahead of time for future storms. I had no idea!

That's the irony of practicing. We have no idea exactly what we are practicing for until we're knee-deep in our suffering. Then it becomes a reality as it did for Job. We learn all too quickly what will sustain us and who will carry us. My hope is that you are practicing, and you know as sure as the sun rises tomorrow that God promises to be your refuge and your rock no matter the strength of your hurricane. And even if God seems distant, you will know the sacred truth that His promises will preserve you even in uncertainty.

Make a list of practices you have built into your life up to this point of fearing God, being intentional about your legacy, and worship. What would you like to do differently?

Consider at least one practice to implement over the next few weeks. Find a Scripture passage to help you remember to embed this truth.

Chapter Three
Tornadoes and Twisted Truth

Eli and Sons: Leading Your Family

> God hath given you one face and you make your-
> self another.
>
> —William Shakespeare, *Hamlet*

One of the trickiest parts of navigating leadership and having influence is also having the responsibility of a family. Some of the hardest lessons we learn come from the place we call home. Whether we are married and have children or single with extended family, close relationships always impact our leadership. We are foolish if we think otherwise. So how do we live and lead between the tensions when things aren't well at home or with other intimate close family relationships? What should that look like?

I am not going to suggest a formula; I'm sorry to disappoint you. I know it is a question that lingers in our minds when a crisis enters our world. Fixing complicated relationships seems impossible. What is the appropriate solution when there is an issue, and how do we make sure we are still able to lead in the way God has asked us to lead?

This may sound rather simplistic, but the reason I am so passionate about the Bible is that from cover to cover there are stories of imperfect human beings. There are stories of dysfunctional relationships on every level. There are families strewn with conflict and challenge. And while we can't necessarily find our specific answer in a particular story, I like to think I can find hope and wisdom tucked away in trying to understand what is taking place and how it might relate to my situation.

Take the story of Eli in 1 Samuel 2, for instance. Scripture doesn't sugarcoat Eli's family. It was a wreck. It says plain and straightforward in verse 12, "Now the sons of Eli were worthless men. They did not know the LORD." Ouch! What a commentary on the family. The word *worthless* doesn't have significant implications; it means they were literally "good for nothing, of no worth especially in regards to righteous behavior."

If you keep reading, we find out all the reasons why Eli's sons were worthless. They were philanderers and dishonest men. They took advantage of their privileged position when the people of Shiloh came to present their offerings by forcefully taking the best choice of meat from the sacrifice. They did not follow God's instructions in practicing this ritual even though there was abundant provision for the priest and his family. The Bible says they "treated the offering of the LORD with contempt" (v. 17).

They were blatant in doing every kind of evil that played into their egotistical desires. They had no regard for the things of God, and here their father was the high priest and judge, the shepherd if you will, for Israel.

The reasoning for all their ungodly behavior? "They did not know the LORD" (v. 12). This is confusing to me. How could they grow up in a godly environment with Eli as their father and not know the Lord? There is no written indication that Eli shirked his duties as a parent. He was a good and godly man. Maybe his crime as a parent was he was too indulgent. He was rebuked later by a man of God who delivered a harsh message to Eli about the future of his descendants (see 1 Samuel 3:11–14). The mom is absent from the picture by the account. We don't know the backstory, and yet we know Eli is deeply grieved by his sons' behavior. It had to have impacted his ability to lead.

As I dug a little deeper, I found the meaning of the word *know* in "they did not know the Lord" in 1 Samuel 2:12. It comes from the root word *yada* in Hebrew and has the meaning of "notice; understand," or to know by experience.

Eli's sons Hophni and Phineas didn't take notice of God in their lives. They weren't familiar with experiences with God. Therefore they did what they wanted and were destructive and an embarrassment to Eli. When Eli confronted them, the Bible says, "But they would not listen to the voice of their father" (v. 25).

They were adults and chose to be belligerent, practicing evil of every kind. They are referred to as "sons of Belial" (v. 12) in the King James Version, an ancient Hebrew name aligned with Satan himself. The word refers to a person who is so utterly full of themselves with pride and envy that they can't submit themselves to anyone over them in a position of authority—a sad legacy for Eli and his family. God decided to end the lineage by putting his two sons to death on the same day as each other.

These men had every access to God, and yet the truth became twisted in their lives. They used what they knew to live in deception and became corrupt as a result.

Eli's family history contained multiple small thunderstorms. And those small storms kept building and gaining the wind of twisted truths. Finally, it turned into a full-scale tornado storm that left a wake of damage for the legacy and influence of the godly priest of Shiloh.

My knowledge of tornadoes came when I was about five years old watching *The Wizard of Oz*. Dorothy lived in Kansas when a tornado sucked up her home and everything she loved on the farm. I watched with wide eyes as chickens, cows, horses, and her family swirled round and round. Dorothy, clutching her bed, watched out the window as she felt her house spinning in the center of the tornado. I was relieved as a child that I didn't live in Kansas, the magical Emerald City or not!

You might say Eli's sons were small thunderstorms of mischief at the start, sucking up their godless behaviors. As they continued in their rebelliousness, the impact of their behavior spread, gaining speed as a wild tornado. They sucked up every sort of godlessness and rained debris for miles, smearing the household name of Eli.

How did Eli continue to serve in his duties, carrying the weight of his unruly sons? Were there whispers behind his back from the people in Shiloh about his parenting and his character? He is acutely aware of the vast swath of destruction his sons are leaving. Did he have someone to talk to in order to relieve his burden and gain encouragement? Did he find himself in moments of despair? How did he find the courage to carry on? These are questions we might ask as we find ourselves in similar situations.

I have a close friend who lives in the heartache of watching her adult child trying to escape the pain of drug addiction. Her son used to often say, "It doesn't matter where I go; God is always in my face." And she said it made him angry. She is an extraordinary, faithful, godly leader, and yet she has a child who hasn't been able to pull out of the vortex of addiction. It has been going on for years. At times she and her husband had to turn him away from their home because he was a danger to them and others. They have worked to help him in every way possible, and yet he has not been able to entirely escape the clutches of the deadly lure of drugs. He is disconnected from God, unable to see that God is the release he is looking for. As I've watched my friend through her years of ministry leadership, I know it has only been because of God's grace that she hasn't collapsed into a heap of despair. I have tremendous respect for her family and every confidence in her parenting.

I remember asking her how she is able to continue in leadership in the capacity she leads. Her response is a quiet reserve, knowing she can only do what God asks of her and leave her son in the capable hands of her loving heavenly Father. Her resilience is a spiritual depth that comes from the kind of suffering of watching someone you love falter. I know she has her moments of crying. I know she wears her floor out pacing and praying. I also know she won't give up as long as she has breath in her body. He is her son, and she loves him.

There are never any guarantees. Just because we take our children to church every Sunday, enroll them in Bible club, and try our best to teach loving Jesus with all our being, they still grow up to be independent adults who make their own decisions. They may choose to know but not live as though they honestly notice God in their lives.

My heart has broken as I've listened and prayed for friends who have had to walk this path, and it is agony as a parent. It's easy to beat yourself up about all the things you could have done differently, and yet at times we just can't figure it out. We don't understand. I wish in those times I had definite answers to give those who trust me to pray for their families.

What is the answer? When our life is at a standstill and we watch those we love being sucked up and swept away in the tornado, what do we do as a leader? What do we do when we don't have control over the winds that blow into our lives and are beginning to create a tornado?

Unfortunately, there are no easy answers. Whether a crisis means a wayward child, a broken marriage, or a dividing chasm in an extended family, each situation warrants careful consideration on how it impacts our ability to lead or continue in leadership.

Sometimes we need to step away. It can be wise to step back and gain clarity and perspective. This isn't an easy decision and shouldn't be done hastily. Whether or not we are the one at fault, feelings of failure can cause us to immediately want to walk away from leading. I am confident Eli had moments when he felt he should resign from his priesthood. I believe there is a pathway of wisdom we need to seek to make those decisions.

When my husband and I separated, I knew I had to step back from my ministry roles for a season. I was speaking several times a year, and at the beginning, I needed to take a chance to get help and sort out with God what was happening in my soul. I needed some intense self-care. I made this decision not out of shame or personal feelings of failure but rather wisdom collected along the way. I knew my pain was too intense, and I wasn't in a place to be able to teach and lead at the same level I had been. My wound was blinding me, and continuing would be a distraction to the healing that was needed.

James 1:5–6 says, "If any of you lacks wisdom, let him ask God, who gives generously to all without reproach, and it will be given him. But let him ask in faith, with no doubting, for the one who doubts is like a wave of the sea that is driven and tossed by the wind." Kevin and I memorized the first chapter of James when we were dating, and I can't tell you how many times it has come to my rescue.

Wisdom says that when a tornado is coming, go to a storm shelter if you have one. If you are in a building or your home and can't get to a shelter, stay away from windows and get to the center of the room. If you are outside, lay flat on the ground, preferably in a ditch so as not to be hit by any debris or sucked into the tornado.

Being wise can shelter us from getting hit with everything spewed out from the situation. Wisdom is our greatest ally in times of crisis to avoid unnecessarily being caught in the tornado and slammed with flying debris. It will lead us to take the careful steps toward solving what we are facing.

Here are some suggestions to keeping out of the path of debris and staying wisely sheltered.

1. Don't be afraid to ask why.

    Well-meaning Bible teachers may have taught us not to ask questions, especially the *why* question. I think this is a mistake. Asking questions puts us in touch with what is happening internally when we face a crisis. It sets us on the path to clean up the debris around us and gain a heart of wisdom. Even Jesus asked God a why question. When He was on the Cross in horrific pain both physically and spiritually, He asked, "My God, my God, why have you forsaken me?" (Matthew 27:46). Why have You abandoned and rejected Me was His heart cry. When we ask God the why question, it evokes another question—what is the purpose or the result of this suffering? It leads us on a journey to once again remember the goodness of God in all things. It brings us to a place where we can worship as Job did when he was struck with calamity. It leads us to a fresh place of humility knowing we can't fix it, God sees the bigger picture, and we can trust Him. Wisdom says it's OK to ask why. We may not like the answer or even get one, but articulating the why question helps us to process.

2. Avoid isolation.

    It is so easy to want to run and hide and separate from others. My encouragement is to create some solitude to think and ask questions, but don't isolate yourself. Solitude is carving out space to pray and reflect. Isolation means you cut yourself off from everyone and everything. That isn't healthy. When we isolate, we set ourselves up for the fiery darts of the enemy. He comes in like a flood to condemn, discourage, and throw our emotions around like a rag doll. We can't lead in crisis in an isolated vacuum. If we isolate, we also put up walls, which hamper our ability to lead. When we isolate, our pain can turn into attitudes that don't serve us well as a leader. When we are alone, our thoughts and anger and resentment seep in, which then cause us to leak. We lead in ways that can hurt others because we are hurting. Isolation fosters inauthenticity. The leaders I admire most are those who are authentic even when they are facing monumental challenges. They are real. And when they are real I want to rally behind them even more. Authentic leaders are leaders who are self-aware and who understand their lives and behavior impacts others.

3.   Seek godly counsel.

The tendency in situations like these as a leader is to try and figure it out ourselves or listen to people who are maybe a little too close to us to be objective. I am not saying those closest to us can't give us godly counsel; I am saying broadening our counsel in times of crises can be wise. The best decision I made during my dark season was to seek godly counsel outside of my church with someone who knew little about my situation or me. They were able to be objective and give insight I was unable to see.

What happens when you are thrust into a crisis in which you have no control? Well-meaning friends can take up an offense for us. It feels good to have someone take up an offense for us and to say things like:

"I don't know how I could forgive someone like that."

"You don't deserve to be treated like that."

"If I were you, I would never go back to that church."

"You should just walk away."

They try to console and comfort us, which isn't a bad idea. We all need support and compassion, but we also need to be asked the tougher questions to help guide us along with empathy. We need people in our lives who will help steer us back to being obedient to God and to keep our integrity in the wake of the storm. We need people who will push us to stay as close to God by staying tethered to His Word and hunkering down in the shelter of prayer even when He seems silent in the storm. It may take a little research to find someone who can help, but it is worth the reward of having a wise counselor to guide you.

4. Enlist support.

The opposite of isolation is to pull up your supporters. Leaders have trouble asking for help. We want to appear competent in all things. When we are hurting, we need extra support. There is no shame in asking for help. I wish we would get this into our thick skulls. Somehow we have bought into the lie that we are to be supportive to everyone else who is in crisis but not to ourselves. In extreme situations, we are forced to enlist support because we can't possibly carry on without it. My suggestion is not to wait for the extreme conditions. Look around you and identify those who can be your support system. Invest in those friends and nurture the relationships. In a time of crisis for either of you, our friends will be Jesus to you and me. In my experience, what I have often discovered is the people you think will be supportive don't come through. There are those on the periphery who come out of the woodwork and become like oxygen when I am gasping for air. Former professional basketball player Magic Johnson is quoted as saying, "When you face a crisis you know who your true friends are."

I found out quickly who my true friends were when Kevin and I separated for those short few months. I don't fault them entirely. There are questions that are hard to answer, and it's OK. I also get it that people sometimes just don't know how to respond. God knows what I need, and He knows what you need when we face a tornado of a crisis.

To lead or not to lead isn't the question in a tornado season because I believe God will give you and me the right answer when we seek His wisdom. The real issue is keeping our perspective in the midst of the falling debris so we can lead with integrity. Tornado chasers keep perspective. These are people who chase tornadoes for a living; they are usually scientists who study weather and want to understand more about these natural disasters. They watch and wait from a distance to record data. Like a tornado chaser, we can wait and watch from a distance when a tornado threatens to drop into our life. Wisdom watches from a distance, keeping perspective of the storm and away from excess debris so we can continue to lead with godly integrity.

Which of the four wisdom principles could you use to help you right now?

Make a list of the people in your life who you can count on for support. What can you do to strengthen these relationships? If you can't name even one, stop right now and pray for God to send you someone who can be a friend and provide godly counsel in a crisis.

Chapter Four

FIRESTORM FALLOUT

Paul and Barnabas: Sharp Disagreements

> Disagreement is part of being a person who has choices. One of those choices is to respect others and engage in intelligent conversation about differences of opinion without becoming enemies, eventually allowing us to move forward to compromise.
>
> —Ben Carson, *One Nation*

In an article written in *Christianity Today*, the story is told of two brothers. The older brother at the latter part of his life wrote the younger brother scolding, "Do not hinder me if you will not help." The younger brother responded, "Perhaps, if you had kept close to me, I might have done better. However, with or without help, I creep on."

These two brothers are familiar to us through the beginnings of the Methodist church—John and Charles Wesley. They had as many similarities as they had disagreements. Both brothers were published poets the same as their father, Samuel Wesley. They were both musicians, and both were ordained in the Church of England, as was their father. Both attended Christ Church at Oxford, and both had a spiritual experience that was significant and led them to create the movement of the Methodists in the eighteenth century. They had divisions in theology, and yet John encouraged they each move forward in their strengths as not to hamper the gospel.

One of their most divisive disagreements came over finding suitable preachers for the practice of outdoor preaching. As the movement grew, there was a growing need for lay preachers. They had outgrown the number of trained clergy from the Anglican Church associated with the Methodist movement. Charles questioned some of the people John chose and disagreed with the general concept of outdoor teaching. John's answer to his brother's objections was to put Charles in charge of vetting the incoming new preachers.

But the problem wasn't solved. The brothers still had vastly different views on the qualifications of the men they vetted. Charles insisted the men should be spiritually appointed with the gift of preaching, and therefore he rigorously tested each candidate. John, however, preferred grace before gifts and was concerned there would be an absence of preachers under his brother's rigors. Their disagreements didn't end there. They also argue over whether or not lay preachers should keep their day jobs or be ordained so they could administer the sacraments. They differed on whether one should be loyal first to the Church of England and then Methodism or Methodism first and then the Church of England. It created a chasm of disagreement that only highlighted their already opposing viewpoints.

Charles's standards to stay faithful to the Church of England implementing Methodism kept the Methodist movement intact. John came to the conclusion that he opposed his brother on this: "You say I separate from the Church. I say I do not. Then let it stand." Because John heeded his brother's concern over this and other issues, the Methodist movement grew. By the nineteenth century, the Methodists were the largest Protestant denomination in the United States.

Disagreements are natural and to be expected. Without conflict, there can be no growth. Business leader and author Patrick Lencioni asserts that one of the five biggest dysfunctions in a team is fear of conflict. In his book, *Overcoming the Five Dysfunctions of a Team*, he says, "Teams that trust one another are not afraid to engage in passionate dialogue around issues and decisions that are key to the organization's success. They do not hesitate to disagree with, challenge, and question one another, all in the spirit of finding the best answers, discovering the truth, and making significant decisions."

Disagreements are healthy. But what happens when the conflict is so divisive that it causes people to part ways? We see this in the story of Paul and Barnabas in Acts 15. They have what the Bible calls a "sharp disagreement" (v. 39). Let's look at the story a little closer and see if we can dissect it to get to the root of the controversy.

> And after some days Paul said to Barnabas, "Let us return and visit the brothers in every city where we proclaimed the word of the Lord, and see how they are."
>
> —v. 36

Paul sounds reasonable and full of potential, desiring to encourage the church. Paul and Barnabas were a great team, and another missionary journey seemed feasible. I am sure they agreed it was a good idea right then and there. They were compatible travelers and connected in one heart and spirit. They agreed in doctrine and purpose of the journey.

> Now Barnabas wanted to take with them John
> called Mark. But Paul thought best not to take with
> them one who had withdrawn from them in Pam-
> phylia and had not gone with them to the work.
>
> —vv. 37–38

John Mark was Barnabas's cousin and had traveled with them on the previous journey but had left early. The Bible doesn't say why; it only says he left. Barnabas was willing to give him another chance, and yet Paul adamantly disagreed.

> And there arose a sharp disagreement, so that they
> separated from each other. Barnabas took Mark
> with him and sailed away to Cyprus, but Paul chose
> Silas and departed, having been commended by
> the brothers to the grace of the Lord.
>
> —vv. 39–40

We have to ask ourselves, is this separation a bad thing? I don't necessarily think so. I am sure they didn't separate hastily. They probably discussed it several times, trying to reconcile their different point of views about who they should take with them. We know they had respect for one another and were committed to the same mission—to see the gospel go into all places. Each had personal convictions and, like the Wesley brothers, had to come to a decision of what would be best for the bigger picture.

My friend Erica Wiggenhorn wrote a Bible study series on the Book of Acts. She shares in her study, *The Unexplainable Church*:

> I'm not suggesting that either was completely with-
> out fault, but for Paul to take John Mark along, he
> would have done so begrudgingly and in a critical
> spirit, serving as a distraction from his message

of grace he was called to deliver. For Barnabas to choose Paul's way over his heart for his cousin quite possibly would have produced deep guilt within Barnabas, distracting him from the message of freedom in Christ he was called to share. So rather than concede one to another, they chose to separate.

Concessions as leaders aren't necessarily bad when you want the same outcome. Both Paul and Barnabas wanted the churches to be strengthened; they desired for the gospel to go out to the cities and towns in the region. They were committed to their doctrine of Jesus coming to bring salvation for all. The method of how they were to continue is what tripped them up. Where Barnabas seemed willing to forgive John Mark, Paul was reluctant and maybe a bit more like Charles Wesley—a little more exacting in nature.

Is it wrong or is it just different? That is the question I think we have to ask ourselves as leaders when we face a disagreement. What I see in this story are a few things I can look at if I find myself in this same situation. I have to ask these questions:

- Does the person I disagree with and I have the same mission?
- Are we committed toward the same results?
- Does the issue conflict or compromise the core doctrine of what I believe to be true from God's Word?
- Is this a personal value conflict?
- Is this about winning or being right?
- Does it matter?
- Is it wrong or is it just different?

Filtering through a set of questions like this can help us evaluate whether or not coming to a compromise would clash against a value we might feel strongly about. In this particular scenario, Paul might have felt as though continuing to mister alongside John Mark would go against a certain standard due to John Mark's failing of the last journey. Maybe he felt John Mark wasn't quite ready to keep up with the rigor of the intensity of ministry. We can only speculate. John Mark drops out of Acts completely at this point, and we don't hear about him until much later.

At the end of the Book of Philemon, Paul refers to John Mark as his fellow worker. Did he have a change of heart? Maybe. He might have needed more time to see John Mark's commitment in order to trust him. Nevertheless, John Mark is the known writer of the second Gospel, the Book of Mark. So whether or not Paul affirmed him for the missionary journey, the gospel did go forth, and the separation created a larger movement.

Barnabas and Paul's incident in the development of the early church probably sparked a fire controversy. We tend to think of fire as negative. And it certainly can be.

I remember a few summers ago driving near my parent's house in the Cleveland National Forest and witnessing miles and miles of charred land where a wildfire had wreaked devastation months earlier. It was unnerving as I imagined the fire raging through that area. Environmentalists, however, say not all fires are bad. Some are good for the earth. Wildfires can be regenerative in nature and bring balance to the ecosystem. When a wildfire happens in the forest, it creates an enormous amount of nutrients in the soil, which bring a flood of new plant growth. It can also increase amounts of plant and animal diversity.

Sometimes a disagreement provides clarity. In the early 1940s there were two up-and-coming itinerant evangelistic preachers—Charles "Chuck" Templeton, a city boy from Toronto, Canada, and Billy Graham, a farm boy from Charlotte, North Carolina. Despite early success, Templeton began to question his faith. This led him on a path that ended in him leaving the ministry and becoming an agnostic.

Templeton challenged his close friend Graham, calling it intellectual suicide to believe the Bible, and specifically the Genesis account, by faith.

Graham had his crisis of belief, as told by his grandson Will, one night by a tree stump in California.

> "O God! There are many things in this book I do not understand. There are many problems with it for which I have no solution. There are many seeming contradictions. There are some areas in it that do not seem to correlate with modern science. I can't answer some of the philosophical and psychological questions Chuck and others are raising."
>
> And then, my grandfather fell to his knees, and the Holy Spirit moved in him as he said, "Father, I am going to accept this as Thy Word—by faith! I'm going to allow faith to go beyond my intellectual questions and doubts, and I will believe this to be Your inspired Word!"
>
> My granddaddy wrote in his autobiography that as he stood up his eyes stung with tears, but he felt the power and presence of God in a way he hadn't in months. "A major bridge had been crossed," he said.

Templeton also writes about his dialogue with the fierce conviction of his friend Graham. In his book, *Farewell to God*, Templeton quotes Graham:

> When I take the Bible literally, when I proclaim it as the Word of God, my preaching has power. When I stand on the platform and say, "God says," or "the Bible says," the Holy Spirit uses me. There are results. Wiser men than you and I have been arguing questions like this for centuries. I don't have the time or the intellect to examine all sides

of each theological dispute, so I've decided, once for all, to stop questioning and accept the Bible as God's Word.

Here the two separated in those early years of their ministries. In this case, they couldn't agree to disagree. It wasn't about asking whether something was wrong or just different when it came to the essentials of the Christian faith. It wasn't about making a concession for the greater good or offering a compromise. These two friends held opposing values, and for Graham to do anything but sever his relationship with Templeton would have kept him from what we know today as one of the greatest evangelists in the history of the last century.

Disagreements, even hot ones, can have a purpose. Like a fire, it can clear away the excess and clean up the dead and decaying debris. In one instance it regenerates, and God can use it to further His purposes. In the other, it can bring clarity of belief for greater anointing in expressing the gifts God has entrusted to us.

As leaders, disagreements can be challenging and can test us. Our level of maturity shows up real fast if we don't practice being gracious, kind, and sensible. I always try to remember I am not the only one who is to be considered during a disagreement. There are others I influence who watch how I choose to handle situations. Coming to a concession while honoring the other person is maturity. Although the Book of Acts doesn't clarify, I believe Paul and Barnabas were mature enough to handle their disagreement with grace. Notice in Acts 15:40, Paul was "commended by the brothers" as they chose to separate. We are presented with the facts, they disagreed, and here are the points of their disagreement. This implies they handled their disagreement well, even though it was a tough situation.

We as leaders always have to remember that no decision impacts only us or the few people we have a disagreement with. It is not only a testing time for us but also a learning classroom for others. It reminds me of a learning lab for upcoming doctors—a surgery room with glass windows with watching residents who take notes on how the surgeon and his team are tackling the very delicate act of restoring someone's health. It's like a theater stage, and others are watching closely.

Keeping our integrity strong in a disagreement requires a few things:

1. Take a step back and think about these questions we looked at earlier.

   - Does the person I disagree with and I have the same mission?
   - Are we committed toward the same results?
   - Does the issue conflict or compromise the core doctrine of what I believe to be true from God's Word?
   - Is this a personal value conflict?
   - Is this about winning or being right?
   - Does it matter?
   - Is it wrong or is it just different?

   Then answer this question: What about the other person's opinion can I affirm?

2. Listen more than you speak.

   When we are in a disagreement, we tend to want to talk more than listen. Simple in concept, it is a practice we need to engage.

3. Stick to the facts.

   Try not to let your emotions take you down a path of making speculations.

4. Find the common purpose.

    Do you both want the same result? Or is this a genuine parting of values?

5. Keep a cool head.

    Emotion driven by anger can sabotage the ability to listen and have constructive dialogue.

6. Take some time to think about it.

    Does it have to be solved in one conversation? Come back to it if either of you gets too heated.

These are not necessarily practices you might not already know as a leader. If you are like me, you may know these things but forget and fall back into bad habits. I offer them as reminders. There are some excellent books on negotiating conflict, and if this is a red flag for you, pick one up and start learning. We can all do better!

One of the biggest issues I have observed in other leaders trying to solve a conflict is allowing their emotions to take them down a path they regret. Heated words are spoken without much thought and emotions derail the real issues. I am sure Paul and Barnabas had emotions flare up from time to time, but I have to believe they kept them in check, allowing them to preserve their influence, otherwise the gospel recordings wouldn't have been so compelling.

So the next time you find yourself in a place of disagreement as a leader, you might think of it as a positive wildfire regenerating your leadership and ministry.

What is your typical reaction to a disagreement? Is it to defend yourself or your ministry?

Where can you find common ground next time to diffuse the sharpness of the disagreement?

Chapter Five
ICE STORMS, ICY SOULS

Esau: Respecting Your Birthright

> One always measures friendships by how they
> show up in bad weather.
>
> —Winston Churchill

Since we get more than our fair share of rain here in the
Pacific Northwest, many of us have collections of raincoats
and rain boots. I have five overcoats in an array of colors and
styles and two pairs of boots. Excessive? Maybe. But when
you spend several days of the year running in and out of the
rain you like to have a creative variation in your rain protection. Our winters can be quite mild and rather dull with
limited change from fall to winter to spring. Just rain and
more rain. On the rare occasion when it gets cold enough
to freeze, sending snow and ice, everything can grind to a
halt, especially when it comes to driving. Our topography
has a fair amount of hills, and the wet roads consequently
turn to sheets of ice, making driving hazardous and unsafe.

I remember one winter as a ten-year-old kid everything
coming to a standstill all around me. At least it seemed
that way. Little did I know it was one of the biggest snowstorms Seattle ever had with nearly fifteen inches of snow
falling in one day and more than forty-seven inches in the
month of January.

We lived at the bottom of a hilly cul-de-sac where ice and cars just don't get along. The parents in our neighborhood decided to park all the cars at the top of the hill to make way for the greatest ice hill ever to be created in the history of our small suburban town. Our schools closed, parents stayed home from work, and we spent days bundled up and sliding down the sheet of ice on our hill. When the snow started to give way in places, the adults continued the fun by pouring water over the exposed spots so our ice adventure could be extended.

There were, however, some safeguards our parents put in place to keep us from ramming ourselves into trees and obstacles. We were to be careful and wear clothing that protected us from getting too wet and cold. We begrudgingly obeyed, and it was worth it. The restrictions kept us within the boundaries of safety.

Just as the adults in my ten-year-old life set guidelines to help keep me safe, there are parameters we as leaders and influencers need to have in place to keep our hearts and integrity in check. Our character is the foundation from which we influence others. We could go to the halls of history and identify men and women who did not finish well due to lack of character. I fear the list would be too many to count. Billy Graham said, "When wealth is lost, nothing is lost; when health is lost, something is lost; when character is lost, all is lost."

Character doesn't erode overnight. The corrosion sneaks in with small compromises, and over time we adopt new patterns. If left unchecked we can suddenly find ourselves at a place of no return.

The wildly popular PBS series *Mr Selfridge* illustrates character compromise and nearly glorifies Harry Selfridge and his crumbling reputation. Selfridge was a retailing genius of the twentieth century. He opened an exclusive city block shopping experience on Oxford Street in London. This type of shopping extravaganza was unheard of in the early 1900s. I have to admit while the series captivated me week after week, I couldn't help but feel sad as I watched him make poor choice after poor choice, which eventually led to his financial and relational demise. The series finishes on a rather more subdued note, not exposing the reality of his failings. In real life, his lack of character—which included compulsiveness, marital affairs, and a gambling addiction—became his undoing. The monumental department store still stands on Oxford Street in downtown London, but Selfridge is remembered as a man who failed in what is most important in life. Walking through the glamorous Selfridge stores this past summer while on a trip to London, I was reminded of what Mr. Selfridge left as his legacy—brokenness, financial destitution, and relational ruin.

Sounds pretty morbid and nearly impossible to keep our character intact and our influence immovable, wouldn't you agree? I would say it's hard, apart from an authentic relationship with Jesus Christ. Why are some people able to keep their character stable and secure while others may start well but end up finishing in a near disaster? What are those necessary safeguards?

Before we try to answer these questions, I want to take us to the story of Esau and Jacob that starts in Genesis 25. Esau and Jacob were born to Isaac and Rebekah. Isaac was Abraham's son, the promise from God who is born to him when he is one hundred years old. He is the first of many descendants who become the nation of Israel and God's chosen people. Rebekah is pregnant with twins, and Esau is born first and then Jacob. They are as different as night and day both in appearance and in temperament. Isaac and Rebekah each favor one son, and the brothers' rivalry is set in motion from the beginning.

One ordinary day Esau came in from the fields, and this is how the story went:

> Isaac loved Esau because he enjoyed eating the wild game Esau brought home, but Rebekah loved Jacob. One day when Jacob was cooking some stew, Esau arrived home from the wilderness exhausted and hungry. Esau said to Jacob, "I'm starved! Give me some of that red stew!" (This is how Esau got his other name, Edom, which means "red.") "All right," Jacob replied, "but trade me your rights as the firstborn son." "Look, I'm dying of starvation!" said Esau. "What good is my birthright to me now?" But Jacob said, "First you must swear that your birthright is mine." So Esau swore an oath, thereby selling all his rights as the firstborn to his brother, Jacob. Then Jacob gave Esau some bread and lentil stew. Esau ate the meal, then got up and left. He showed contempt for his rights as the firstborn.
>
> —Genesis 25:28–34 NLT

A few chapters later we find Isaac dying, and as was customary, the elder of the home would give a blessing to his children starting with the firstborn. Rebekah got word of this and because she favored Jacob, talked him into disguising himself as Esau so he would receive the firstborn blessing from his father.

Esau returned and is preparing food for his father to receive his blessings, and this is what he encountered:

> But Isaac asked him, "Who are you?" Esau replied, "It's your son, your firstborn son, Esau." Isaac began to tremble uncontrollably and said, "Then who just served me wild game? I have already eaten it, and I blessed him just before you came. And yes, that blessing must stand!" When Esau heard his father's words, he let out a loud and bitter cry. "Oh my father, what about me? Bless me,

too!" he begged. But Isaac said, "Your brother was here, and he tricked me. He has taken away your blessing." Esau exclaimed, "No wonder his name is Jacob, for now, he has cheated me twice. First, he took my rights as the firstborn, and now he has stolen my blessing. Oh, haven't you saved even one blessing for me?"

—Genesis 27:32–36 NLT

Can't you sense the agony in Esau's cry? He not only carelessly sold his birthright for a bowl of stew, but he is cheated out of his father's blessing reserved for the firstborn son.

Our North American culture can't fathom the significance of both the birthright and the blessing; we don't practice these as such. The birthright in the Jewish culture is of great importance because it involves passing on the authority in a family over the household and the property with all that the family owns. In biblical times the firstborn was usually given a double portion of the estate. It also symbolized the blessing that would put the firstborn in close favor and covenant relationship with God.

In the lives of both brothers, patterns of deceitfulness and competition continue from that day forward. And those patterns were already set in motion by their parents and grandparents. Chapters earlier, both Abraham and Isaac were deceptive when asked about their wives masquerading as brother and sister rather than as husband and wife (see Genesis 12; 20; and 26).

Reading between the lines, it isn't too difficult to figure out how the rivalry between the brothers happened. Their heated competitiveness was the result of parents favoring one child over another. Imagine the games they played just to keep the peace. These character patterns formed in dysfunction and were allowed to thrive, which created havoc for the generations to follow. Jacob's life was defined by his deceit and Esau's soul grew embittered through the years. The good news is the brothers eventually reconciled (see Genesis 32—33), but they stayed separated for most of their lives.

Even if we are raised in an overly dysfunctional home, there is hope as we submit our hearts to God. We can ask Him to help us keep aware of those things that might lead us to character deficits, creating an icy soul.

I propose five ways to safeguard our character to keep our influence immovable. This list isn't exhaustive, and you might come up with your own ways. Peeking into the story of Jacob and Esau, we can observe what was missing and help establish these five safety checks to make sure we aren't headed in the same direction.

1. Respect Your Birthright

Esau didn't value his birthright. He quickly exchanged it for a moment of physical contentment. This isn't a whim of a choice feigning contempt toward his birthright because he is hungry. Yes, it is a compulsive decision, and if he had valued his birthright in the first place, he wouldn't have so easily given it up. It had to have been in the back of his mind. Esau had utter disregard for his birthright.

What is our birthright? Our birthright is our position in Christ, not the standing in our birth family. Rather it is our spiritual status, the righteousness of God, which Jesus imputed to us through His death on the Cross. We don't take it for granted.

I have to admit that sometimes I take my spiritual birthright for granted. My spiritual journey has been influenced by a long and extensive godly heritage. I was born into a Christian family, and all I have ever known is Jesus and faith. I owned it for myself as a young thirteen-year-old girl by a fireside event at camp. I chose to surrender everything to follow Jesus, and God has been in my life ever since I can remember. Not that I haven't wrestled long and hard or had painful experiences. I certainly struggle, but I know in my heart that Jesus is always an option for me to consider. It is a choice I make to activate my faith in steering my character. As a result, I work to make choices every single day to value my birthright by spending time reading God's Word, exercising my relationship with God through prayer, loving others well, and intentionally trying to make decisions the best I know how that would please Him. When I don't choose this route, it is when, like Esau, I devalue my birthright and make compulsive choices—and believe me there are those unfortunate days. But I am humbly learning the more I value my heritage, the stronger I forge my character.

It only takes one impulsive moment to disregard our birthright as Esau did. And then we have to live with the regrets that can change the trajectory of our lives. Cultivating and valuing our birthright is paramount to keeping our character safe and secure.

2. Be Accountable

We can't do life alone, and if we isolate we remove ourselves from the possibilities of living a full life and experiencing the beauty of community. We miss learning and growing with others. You can't learn in a vacuum. That's called acquiring knowledge. It's not what we learn in private that helps us grow—it's taking what we learn and practicing it with our community of family, friends, church, work, and those we encounter every single day. Accountability isn't just about asking one person to hold us to a particular behavior or belief. Accountability is living out our lives openly with others and allowing those closest to us to help us grow and change by practicing humility and being teachable. Community is a safeguard that keeps our character on track.

Even with community, sometimes it is healthy to engage a personal mentor to hold us accountable. At the beginning of this year, I realized in order to move forward with some things I was wrestling with in my character, I needed to have someone other than friends and family hold me accountable. I found it essential to take steps to go to a deeper level. I prayed for what seemed like a long time, and finally, God opened up a life-giving relationship for me. She doesn't live nearby, but our goal is to video chat about once a month. She asks me hard questions and challenges my thinking. I am encouraged to keep pushing through unresolved feelings and not to accumulate lingering hurts. Most of all, she has committed to pray for me. I can't tell you enough how incredibly meaningful that commitment is. As a leader of leaders, I've been that person for others. And sometimes it is hard to make time and space for that experience. It is highly necessary! I encourage you. No, I *challenge* you as a leader and an influencer to find someone in your life who can help be the safeguard to keep your character moving in the right direction.

3. You Are Who You Hang Out With

My mother used to tell me over and over again when I was a teenager: I would become who I hung out with. I shrugged and passed over her advice and then found out the hard way—it really was really true. I learned a valuable lesson when I missed the last football game of the season and the big party celebration. I allowed a friend to talk me into disregarding my parents' curfew the week before. I remember sitting in the kitchen, miserable as can be, pulling all my manipulative teenage promises of how sorry I was, hoping one of them would give in and let me go. They stuck to their decision, and I am glad they did. I learned to make wise choices and fewer compromises.

This same principle is valid for adults. If you and I want to have immovable influence that doesn't bend on a whim or compromise when the going gets tough, we have to hang out with people of strong character and integrity. It's not a bad idea to follow them around and study their lives. One of the ways I've done this is to try and read biographies of people who have been influencers and world changers. Peering into the window of such lives as Hannah More, William Wilberforce, Eric Liddell, Gladys Aylward, and others inspire me as I read about the challenges they faced and how their character, defined by their faith, sustained them in the seasons of triumph and hardship.

Esau didn't follow this safeguard. He chose not only to hang out with the wrong crowd, but he also married two Hittite women. The Bible says his wives "made life bitter for Isaac and Rebekah" (Genesis 26:35), while the King James Version translates it as, "Which were a grief of mind unto Isaac and Rebekah." Why did they make life so painful and grievous for Isaac and Rebekah? Because the Hittites served other gods and worshipped idols. These daughters-in-law didn't share the same values Esau had grown up with, and they weren't raised to worship the one true God Jehovah, which probably created some tense family moments.

Those we choose to spend the majority of our time with influence our thinking and behavior. I am not suggesting we only hang out with people who only believe as we do. We are also called to be salt and light in the world (Matthew 5:13–16), our neighborhoods, schools, workplaces, and communities. Association has to do with who we choose to primarily align ourselves with and what values they embrace. As a leader, it is exceptionally important because others are watching—whether we are aware of it or not. They are taking cues from every part of our lives, not just when we are leading.

An old Welsh saying (sometimes attributed to George Bernard Shaw) goes like this: "I learned long ago never wrestle with a pig. You get dirty. And besides, the pig likes it." Remember what my mother said—you are who you hang out with!

4. Keep High Standards

Another safeguard is to adopt the highest standards we possibly can, guided by biblical principles—integrity, respect, honesty, responsibility, and dependability. The list could go on. While culture often praises the very things God labels detestable, as people of immovable influence, we need to keep and practice high standards. Others are watching, and we have to demonstrate by living out the values that matter.

I am not talking about perfection. I am speaking about keeping high standards so others can have confidence and trust in our ability to lead. It gives them a mark to reach for in their lives. It is a motivator for success in a family, on the job, and in our churches. We all need people to look up to and admire. Our youth need role models with unwavering virtues. Our children need moms and dads who choose to demonstrate a life lived for God by example. Our churches need leaders who lead with integrity and humility. Our country needs leaders who are honest and truthful. When we practice high standards, we become something more to follow than empty success. We become people of high character worth emulating.

Esau's family lacked exceptional standards in character. Patterns of lying, manipulation, dishonesty, lack of loyalty, and loss of unity lowered the standards for even this important biblical historical family.

No family is perfect. We all have some dysfunction, and it is with God's help and his exposure of our character deficits that we can work to overcome them. We make mistakes. We are human. Part of godly character is to own our mistakes and correct them as best we can. Understanding our values from God's perspective can help us ensure we keep high standards using God's Word, which is unshakable, as a measurement of character.

Second Peter 1:5–8 (NIV) gives us a list of virtues to keeping high standards:

> For this very reason, make every effort to add to your faith goodness; and to goodness, knowledge; and to knowledge, self-control; and to self-control, perseverance; and to perseverance, godliness; and to godliness, mutual affection; and to mutual affection, love. For if you possess these qualities in increasing measure, they will keep you from being ineffective and unproductive in your knowledge of our Lord Jesus Christ.

Notice how the list is an equation of adding one virtue to the next, and it starts with our faith. Our faith is the foundation of our character and the building block to developing strong, immovable influence. If we just started with this list, we would well be on our way to keeping the foundation of our character strong and stable.

5. Say No to Compromises

The last safeguard is to commit to not compromise the values in the foundation of our character. Compromising actions don't occur overnight. Small temptations turn into small compromises. A series of small compromise turns into an unstoppable wave of compromise that can destroy our character.

"It won't hurt to do this just once. I won't do it again."

"I've been hurt; I deserve this."

"No one will notice."

"It's not that big of a deal."

"It wasn't a lie, and it was partially true."

These are all the whispers of the voice of compromise. The temptation to sacrifice for a brief moment can lead to something more seriously notable in the future.

Because of Esau's and Jacob's compromises, thousands of lives are impacted. Esau's descendants, the Edomites, would become lifelong enemies of God's chosen children, the Israelites. They fought bloody battles. They refused to let Jacob's children pass through their land. Esau's descendant, Herod, had the male infants of Bethlehem killed because he felt threatened by the Christ Child. Little compromises over time turned into a future of separation from God for generations.

Too often character can become our downfall if we don't have safety checks in place. At the closing days of the 2016 Olympics in Rio de Janeiro, Brazil, the games became tainted with the story of US swimmer Ryan Lochte. He is one of the most successful swimmers and has won twelve

Olympic medals in his career. During the 2016 Olympics, Lochte initially claimed men posing as police officers late one night had robbed him and three other US swimmers at gunpoint. Days later, as an investigation ensued, the story took a different turn. It was discovered that Lochte and his teammates were drunken vandals and had been confronted by security guards at a gas station. Later, when he returned to the United States, he was asked in a TV interview if he had been lying. He replied, "I wasn't lying to a certain extent, I over-exaggerated what was happening to me." This one lapse of character and his actions caused damage to the Brazilian hosts and hurt not only his reputation but also the reputation of his teammates. Was this a one-time lapse of character, or did the small compromises begin earlier? Sadly, it left a tarnished mark for the US swim team and the 2016 Olympic Games.

In contrast, another athlete, Eric Liddell, became a champion runner while at the University of Edinburgh, and he competed in the 1924 Paris Olympics. The son of missionaries to China, Eric's devotion to his faith was resolute, and after college he planned to return to China to continue his parents' work. Driven by his convictions he withdrew from the 100-meter race, his best event, which was scheduled to run on a Sunday. He couldn't be persuaded at any cost to compromise his conviction to not work on the Sabbath. He was determined and stood by his decision. Instead, Eric trained for the 400-meter race, which was much more difficult for him. He ended up winning gold for Britain. After, he stayed true to his calling and went to China to become a missionary serving the poor. He wasn't lured by fame or fortune; his godly character guided his actions. His life ended in 1943 at just 43 years of age when he died in an internment camp during the Japanese aggression in China. Eric Liddell's legacy is far reaching, and his life inspires me to remember that paying attention to my character is what steers my influence.

We can learn from the story of Jacob and Esau of what not to do by respecting our spiritual birthright, keeping accountable, choosing our friends wisely, keeping high standards, and saying no to even the smallest of compromises. Attending to our character helps us avoid developing a numbing, icy layer on our hearts that accelerates our loss of influence.

We would be wise to remember to stand firm with immovable influence is to safeguard our character. It is our destiny, and we must protect it with everything we have, not only for ourselves but also for the generations that follow.

Take a minute to write down what is most important to you. What values do you consider critical to keeping your character strong?

Where have you let in small compromises? Talk to God about it, and ask Him which safeguards you need to put in place to say no to compromise. Don't miss this step. Write it down and look at it often.

Chapter Six
LIGHTNING LEARNING
Timothy: Intentional Learning

Anyone who stops learning is old, whether at twenty or eighty. Anyone who keeps learning stays young.

—Henry Ford

The path of spiritual growth is a path of lifelong learning.

—M. Scott Peck, *The Road Less Traveled*

Park Ranger Roy Sullivan is listed in *The Guinness Book of World Records* as the person struck by lightning more recorded times than any other human being. Between 1942 and 1977, he was struck a total of seven times. His first attack shot through his leg, and it wasn't until twenty-seven years later that he was hit for the second time, burning his eyebrows off, lighting his hair on fire, and rendering him unconscious. The other five times included searing his shoulder in his front yard, his hair catching on fire twice more (he even began to keep a bucket of water in his truck in the event he was struck by lightning and needed to douse his head), injuring his ankle, and then the last time burning his chest and stomach. He is referred to as the "Human Lightning Rod."

I've always been in awe of thunderstorms with lightning. Each second there are about 100 lightning discharges. Every day there are 44,000 thunderstorms that move across the planet, and there can be as many as 2,000 in progress at anymoment. That's a lot of lightning discharging a powerful amount of electricity!

Would you like to be attracted to lightning? Not in the literal sense of course. But drawn to the lightning power source of God Himself? Thunderstorms are some of the most powerful storms on earth, and the lightning that accompanies the storm is said to be dangerous because of its power. What would it look like to be dangerously powerful for God?

As leaders and influencers, we have the capacity to discharge powerful amounts of information and truth as we lead. The more truth we understand and, I might add, practically apply to our lives, the better we become in our leadership. The better we become at leading, the more transformation can happen in others. When change happens in people's lives, lightning power is dispersed. We can bring a "flash" of Holy Spirit truth in a much-needed moment with others.

Lightning is not only dangerous it is also unpredictable. With God's power we have the capability of dangerously impacting our world with His truth charged by the Holy Spirit's powerful current. This doesn't happen randomly like lightning in a thunderstorm. We have to be intentional in our learning so the discharge of what we've learned has depth and meaning and the current of power can reach as far as possible.

If we want to strive to be excellent leaders who discharge powerful flashes of truth, then we can't stop stirring up our love for learning. To keep ourselves challenged we have to be intentional about our development, and that includes looking for ways to continually position ourselves to learn. Deciding we don't need to learn anything else is the death of our effectiveness as a leader. If we want to make it through a storm intact, learning helps to anchor us along the way.

Paul charged Timothy in this way to "Fan into flame the gift of God, which is in you" (2 Timothy 1:6). *The Message* translates it this way, "And the special gift of ministry you received when I [Paul] laid hands on you and prayed—keep that ablaze!"

Timothy was Paul's protégé, and Paul was instructing Timothy to be intentional about developing what is entrusted to him. Paul commended Timothy in the previous verse for his sincere faith that was passed on to him by his mother and his grandmother. Now Paul is reminding him that he needs to stir it up. The phrase "fan into flame" actually means to rekindle or resuscitate. The charge is to go back again and stir up the gifts God gave Timothy.

For you and me, the phrase "fan into flame" implies we have to work at our gifts, and we have to continually refresh ourselves by learning to be effective. The origin of words is important here and includes paying attention to the word *flame*, which infers a fire that is hot and ablaze. The figurative sense would be a burning passion. We can't get to the level of discharging a fire that is ablaze unless we stir it up as Paul encouraged Timothy. He doesn't say specifically how Timothy was to do it, but we can speculate that Paul had trained him on what it might look like both in learning and in exercising his gifts.

God gives us all gifts, and gifts don't just develop passively. We have to be intentional about it. We don't turn into effective leaders by osmosis. Notice I am choosing the phrase *effective leader* rather than *successful leader*. We might have a tremendous amount of success as a leader, and yet it is our effectiveness that makes the impact. I would go so far as to say that our effectiveness is directly connected to our ability to learn continually.

So what does keeping our gifts ablaze look like? First of all, we can get a few ideas from the metaphor Paul gives here in 2 Timothy 1:6, "fan into flame." When we think of fanning into flame, it gives the idea of wind that blows on the embers of a fire. *Rekindling* is another word that provides us with the imagery.

Growing up, one of my family's favorite pastimes was camping, and one of the first things my dad taught us was how to build a fire. He showed us to start with small pieces of dry twigs and branches. He then showed us how to blow on the embers and gradually add the rest of the larger kindling. Finally, the wood kept the fire burning. Each morning and each evening he showed us how to rekindle the fire by blowing on the embers and then adding more fuel until we had a fire for cooking and keeping warm.

When we come to Christ, the Holy Spirit ignites our faith and the burning fire within us. We add small pieces of learning, and the fire within us grows. The Holy Spirit gives us gifts, and we then blow on them by learning more, and we begin to use them. We start to see the results of the fire growing, and as we use our gifts more and more, we see the flashes of lightning make its impact.

Here comes the greatest temptation. As we serve in a larger capacity with our gifts and begin to see results, we get tempted to keep the fire going by routine. We might still have passion, but it is not the burning passion we once had. We have enough knowledge under our belts, and the system works for a while. At some point, we are simply throwing the necessary fuel on the fire, and we are not going back again to rekindle. Everything stays the same, and at some point, we become stagnant. We lose our edge, our effectiveness. We can be tempted to let our heads swell because of our success and not think we need to learn any longer.

Antoni Cimolino, artistic director of the Stratford Shakespeare Festival, insists, "There is something to be learned every day, both by looking in the mirror at yourself and by looking at the people around you."

I believe this is more than true, and it has everything to do with what we think of ourselves and whether we believe we need the power of the gospel in our lives or not. The power of the gospel in our lives drives us to want to learn. When we realize we are in need of constant mercy, we start to get a clue. When we see our brokenness and realize we are righteous only in Christ, we are motivated to keep learning, to be more like Jesus in every way.

Paul calls Timothy to a higher standard than to just keep the flame burning. He says, "Fan into flame," which, as we've already talked about, means to stir up, put more fuel on to get that fire burning hotter and hotter. What can happen to us when we see our gifts growing is we can get too comfortable. Our gifts grow, and others start asking us to help them. There is nothing wrong in mentoring others, in fact, we should be doing that, but we still need to continue to learn ourselves.

Another temptation of getting too comfortable is an unwillingness to try something new or learn a new skill. We can let fear get the best of us. It is natural to stay where we are because we can be in control. Pushing ourselves, change, and learning can be scary to put it simply. Paul understood this and tells Timothy, "For God gave us a spirit not of fear but of power and love and self-control" (v. 7). What happens when we get too comfortable with our gifts? We depend less on God and more on our familiar routines and ourselves. We get too busy serving God. We know how the fire is built, and therefore the system works and is comfortable. We just kindle the fire rather than rekindle. Stretching ourselves by learning and growing can be frightening because at some point we have to figure out how to implement what we are learning, and that takes effort.

As we seek to be mature in Christ, the fire has to be rekindled over and over again by continuing to grow and learn in truth, adding more fuel to keep the fire burning. If we stop adding fuel to the fire, we stop learning, the fire might linger, but it will eventually burn out as we stop learning. Learning is essential if we are to stand strong in a storm and keep our influence intact.

What should we be learning? I would answer our capacity for intentional learning should be both personal and professional with a greater emphasis on personal development. For Christ followers that means there are no shortcuts in seeking to develop greater intimacy with Jesus. Now, what I am going to say is nothing new. Our learning has to start and end in the covers of God's Word and in prayer. Nothing stirs up and fans the flame to serve the kingdom as the Word of God does—not to mention what it does for the soul!

There are times, if I am honest, I feel so out of sync and burdened running around doing all my important "leadership stuff" that I forget my most important learning comes from a disciplined time with God. This is what sustains you and me in life and keeps us motivated to keep the fires ablaze. It is and will always be a mystery that in quieting my soul and reading God's Word something significantly powerful takes place in my heart and all is right in the world again. God's Word is truly alive as Hebrews 4:12 clearly reminds us, "For the word of God is living and active, sharper than any two-edged sword, piercing to the division of soul and of spirit, of joints and of marrow, and discerning the thoughts and intentions of the heart."

I am a passionate person, and I am learning at this moment not to be governed by my emotions. The discipline of filling my mind with God's Word over and over again and speaking it out to Him helps me get through whatever I am facing. It also helps me better exercise the role I have been entrusted with.

I think it's important to note here that everyone learns differently, and that's OK. I don't believe there are one-size-fits-all learning processes. We must discover how we learn and effectively integrate that process into our lives. Some of us had negative school experiences. Maybe a teacher spoke harsh words over you and dimmed your motivation. Ever since, it is has been difficult to want to learn. My husband Kevin is one of those people. He didn't have a positive grade school experience, and so when he entered college, he especially struggling with reading and writing. Because he had a professor who took the time to help him, today he is one of the most self-disciplined learners I know. He reads constantly and often has several books going at once. He not only reads them but he also journals what he is learning and seeks to apply it to his life and ministry.

Neil Fleming and Colleen Mills, both of Lincoln University in New Zealand, have identified four ways people learn. See if you can find yourself in one of these descriptions that come from their VARK learning styles:

Visual Learners see information and visualize the relationship between ideas. They love to learn from information in maps, charts, graphs, flow charts, and diagrams. If you want to appeal to a visual learner, the more diagrams the better.

Aural/Auditory Learners hear information and learn best by listening to lectures, participating in group discussions and talking things through because they tend to verbalize their learning.

Read/Write Learners enjoy all forms of reading and writing. They learn best through words. They enjoy PowerPoint presentations, the Internet, journaling, dictionaries, quotes, etc.

Kinesthetic Learners learn best by experience. They use all their senses to engage in learning. Videos and movies of real-life examples help the kinesthetic learner to gather information. They also learn by hands-on experiences.

This is just a brief overview of these learning styles, and no one person learns by one method. You may find you are a combination of one or more of these styles, but one may be dominant.

As I was writing this chapter, I went to the VARK website (vark-learn.com), and completed their free questionnaire, which helps identity your learning style. I thought I was primarily a read/write learning style with a little bit of visual as well, but I scored higher in the auditory and kinesthetic categories. When I read some of the ways these learning styles work, it made sense to me as I related to their assessment of how I learn best and what motivates me. It tells me why I am drawn to conferences and books—it has to do with my learning style.

Once you've discovered the best way, it's important to integrate your learning style into your life in such a way that puts the right kindling on your fire, meaning, adding your gifts to the way you connect to the Holy Spirit in order to discharge His gifts in a lightning-powerful way. The key is just to do it!

If you are finding yourself stagnating and feeling as though you are in a routine in your leadership, it's probably been a while since you have learned anything new. Figure out what energizes you, and make a plan to incorporate some learning into your life on a regular basis. Pray and seek God. Ask Him to show you how to make a plan on what learning will look like in the next several months. Choose a book, attend a seminar, or sign up for a demonstration or hands-on experience that will enhance your learning.

Fear is one of the biggest obstacles of not only using our gifts as Paul is charging Timothy here in this passage but also learning how to use our gifts. God has given us not a spirit of fear, but of sound mind. It all starts in the mind, which is what ultimately keeps us from learning.

We have to mentally move ourselves to a posture of learning, which means we have to admit we need to learn. Some of us have the desire to know more than others. It is how we are wired. It can also be shaped by our experiences in school—whether it was positive or negative. I vividly remember a teacher I had in third grade, and her style of teaching didn't motivate me to want to learn. She seemed angry most of the time, was abrupt, and didn't seem to demonstrate much care for us as her students. Fortunately, most of my teachers were the opposite, and I had a positive learning experience. However, if you had more of a negative experience, don't let that stop you from trying to learn!

I teach part-time in an adult learning classroom for adults finishing their degrees. Many come into the program and haven't been in school for years, sometimes decades. Many of them admit they are fearful. What are they afraid of? Failing, not getting it right, humiliating themselves in front of others, or all of the above. Many of them bring in the baggage of bad learning experiences. Once I reassure them it's OK to experiment and even fail, their fears relax, and they realize that we are learning in a whole different way. It changes the way they learn, and it opens up a whole new world for them.

I often ask them what they are afraid of. I then encourage them to follow the what, the whys, and then more whats and whys of those fears, which then follow to finally verbalizing deep down they do want to learn to transform their lives. Learning brings about transformation and initiates change in us. When fueled with the power of the Holy Spirit, the lightning power of effective leadership takes place

If you want to be able to keep your influence immovable and stand strong in a storm, then learning is a necessary element to staying anchored in Jesus. Our attitude to learn and how we apply what we learn prepares us for the next storm we might face. Our willingness to learn with humility is the ballast that keeps us centered and our leadership intact.

Gordon MacDonald, in his book, *Building Below the Waterline*, makes this astute observation, "The forming of the soul that it might be a dwelling place for God is the primary work of the Christian leader. This is not an add-on, an option, or a third-level priority. Without this core activity, one almost guarantees that he or she will not last in leadership for a lifetime, or that what work is accomplished will become less and less reflective of God's honor and God's purposes."

Our willingness to lean in and learn becomes the formation of our soul. The result is the vast expanse of our heart, which invites God in, and His power is delivered. You could say, the thunderstorm rumbles and the current of a powerful spiritual lightning charge are released when we are willing to learn. I guess we can be attracted to lightning after all!

What best describes your desire to learn?

Which of the four VARK learning styles do you think applies to you? Determine what you can do to challenge your ability to learn.

Chapter Seven
TROPICAL STORM TESTING
Tabitha: Resurrecting Dead Dreams

> There will be obstacles. There will be doubt-
> ers. There will be mistakes. But with hard work,
> with belief, with confidence and trust in yourself
> and those around you, there are no limits.
>
> —Michael Phelps, *No Limits*

Tabitha "was full of good works," which we find in Acts
9:36. She is the only woman in the New Testament specifically called a disciple of Jesus Christ. When she suddenly
becomes ill and dies, there was a swarm of mourners
near her body. Peter was sent an urgent message to come
quickly, indicating Tabitha may have been close to Peter.
When Peter arrived, grieving widows presented Peter and
the disciples with garments Tabitha made for them. These
were the evidence of her good works and her care for the
poor and needy. She was well loved, and her death is a
tremendous loss for the people in the seaport of Joppa.
But Peter performed a miracle through God's spirit, and
Tabitha was restored to life. Word spread quickly about
this one event, and many came to believe.

Tabitha's influence was evident through her mourners—their profound loss and their evidence of the tangible
way Tabitha ministered to them. It seems Tabitha could
have continued to have great influence in her area. Why

did she have to die in the first place? This is a mystery at times why God decides to remove someone in the middle of what seems to be a moment of greatest usefulness. We may get removed for unknown (at least to us) reasons, but nevertheless there is an abruptness in what we are working toward. We may be working diligently, sacrificing everything for God's kingdom following the dream we believe He has whispered to us, and then it happens.

The dream is crushed.

Circumstances change.

The direction is altered.

We are left wondering if we heard God right in the first place. We all know the pat answer of Romans 8:28 when someone with good intentions reminds us that because God loves us there will be good, yes even in the storm that seems to wipe us out. When people throw out verses like lofty platitudes, they don't offer much comfort. It leaves much to be desired. People want to encourage us, and yet I sometimes find these become trite sayings that give little thought to the receiver. No disrespect intended, but let's read Romans 8:28, along with the two verses that precede it, in their entirety before we spout off a few well-meaning words to a hurting friend. I like the way *The Message* puts it.

> Meanwhile, the moment we get tired in the waiting, God's Spirit is right alongside helping us along. If we don't know how or what to pray, it doesn't matter. He does our praying in and for us, making prayer out of our wordless sighs, our aching groans. He knows us far better than we know ourselves, knows our pregnant condition, and keeps us present before God. That's why we can be so sure that every detail in our lives of love for God is worked into something good.
>
> —Romans 8:26–28

Now that is comforting! It doesn't tilt in the direction of a sweet, trite sentiment. It has depth and resonates with my soul. I believe God doesn't send down meaningless and empty spiritual words. He gives us what we need in the context of our disappointment. God wants us to be encouraged with His truth, but He is not unfeeling and hurtful when we hurt. The ESV says in verse 26, "Likewise the Spirit helps us in our weakness." The word *likewise* causes me to go back even further, starting in vs. 24; "For in this hope we were saved. Now hope that is seen is not hope. For who hopes for what he sees? But if we hope for what we do not see, we wait for it with patience." Doesn't that just blow your mind?

I wonder if Peter said something like this to the grieving women surrounding Tabitha to give them hope and not simply tell them God had a purpose in their loss of Tabitha. (Which of course we know He did as we read further along in the story.) The women wailing around her lifeless body knew what death meant—it was final. They were widows, after all, and had experienced it firsthand in their families. Widows were often left to fend for themselves in a culture that didn't honor women or take care of them. Did Peter mention to them, even though they couldn't see the hope of embracing their beloved Tabitha, the time would come when they would see her again?

When you or I happily move along working at a leadership dream God has given us and it gets interrupted to the point of near death, what do we do? How do we stand strong when we can't see the future and it seems as though, like Tabitha, we are taken right out of our usefulness for God?

I don't pretend to know why and how God plans behind the scenes. It can seem utterly wasteful to allow the crushing death of a dream. And yet we know God sees the bigger picture, and we can't fathom all the hows and whys of the future of a dream He entrusted to us in the first place.

When a tropical storm hits, it can hit hard and leave a wake of devastation. It can take the heart right out of a community. We've watched from the comfort of our living rooms the aftermath of tropical storms that have ravaged such countries such as Haiti, Fiji, Puerto Rico, Australia, and parts of Southern Asia. And yet I marvel at the resilience of the human spirit, to pick up and rebuild—to stand up in the rubble and be inspired to restore what was lost.

There was a tropical storm called Cyclone Tracy that hit the town of Darwin, Australia, on Christmas Eve and Christmas Day in 1974. Even though the residents had been warned of the incoming storm, they were taken surprise by its severity. The news spread on December 22 that the path of the storm had headed north and Darwin didn't seem to be a threat. Everyone relaxed. That all changed on December 24 when the storm moved in a different direction, and Darwin became the new target. Because Darwin had experienced other cyclones, many residents believed the city wouldn't be impacted. They couldn't have been more wrong. The storm moved in with a fury, and the city was flattened. Nearly 41,000 of the 47,000 residents ended up homeless, and 70 percent of homes and buildings were destroyed. And yet the determination of the Darwin residents who wanted to rebuild was admirable. By 1978, most of the area had recovered, and they were able to house as many people as before the storm hit. They saw what they couldn't see in the aftermath—a city rebuilt and flourishing once again. And their dream came true in the years that followed.

As leaders and influencers who believe in a sovereign God, we take hope in the faith chapter, Hebrews 11. We are reminded of putting our faith in the assurance of things not seen. God believes in the dreams He gives us, and

He promises to help us stand up in the resurrection of the dream. When we are in this place, we can feel as though God forgets us. We can become disillusioned.

In his book *New Morning Mercies*, Paul David Tripp reminds us, "Our problem is not that God is inactive or that he has abandoned us, but that we are not on his agenda page. Left with confusion about his plan and carrying with us unrealistic expectations, we get disappointed and a little bit cynical, and we quit running to him for help. It is a bit of a spiritual mess."

We will be tested. We will be challenged, even when grieving the loss of what we had expected. Here is how we can stand strong and make sure we are running to God for help.

Hope in what you can't see.

Change your perspective. Don't hope only in what you can physically see with your eyes. Write down the hope you can't see. Record it in your Bible or a journal or both. Date your entry and believe God will answer. Confidently expect, just as God came through for David, Elijah, Moses, Esther, Nehemiah, and others, He will come through for you. He will reveal new hope for the dream He has given you. Jeremiah 29:11 is a timeless promise that reminds us God will not abandon His plans for us: "For I know the plans I have for you, declares the LORD, plans for welfare and not for evil, to give you a future and a hope."

Hang on with patience.

Romans 8:25 says, "But if we hope for what we do not see, we wait for it with patience." Patience is the power to endure stress even in the middle of your dream being crushed. Patience with perseverance is to have the fortitude to hang on and trust in what you can't see.

Surrender what you can't control.

You and I will stand strong in the midst of the whipping winds of a tropical storm if we can yield to that which we can't change. Don't sing the song of the what ifs. Don't be tempted to cave into despair. Grieve if you must for you must grieve. We can't ignore the loss, and grieving is normal. Don't let anyone tell you differently.

We need to take time to grieve even the small losses in our lives. We live in a world where grieving is considered a waste of time. Give it a day or two and move on. That is the message. We can overspiritualize losses if we are not careful. Yes, we are to claim God's promises and, yes, we are to trust God, but pain and loss are real, and they are vital to our spiritual and emotional health.

God created us with the broad range of emotions, and to deny them is to be dishonest with ourselves. The Book of Psalms shows how David expressed his feelings of grief, loss, anger, and sadness—all the way to joy and exaltation. When you have grieved for a time, surrender your pain and know your suffering is just for a little while. First Peter 5:10 says, "And after you have suffered a little while, the God of all grace, who has called you to his eternal glory in Christ, will himself restore, confirm, strengthen, and establish you."

Pray. Pray some more.

Pray when it's hard to pray. Pray when you don't feel like it. This can be a time when you will want to shut God out because you don't understand why your plans have been stopped. This is the time to lean in and pray. It can be hard to find the words to pray in the midst of suffering. If you can't seem to find the words, find someone to pray with you and for you. There have been seasons in my life when all I could utter before God was, "Help!" I have lain flat on my face or on my knees in silence before Him because what I was carrying was so deep. I had to reach out to have others help me in my weakness. Believe that as Romans 8:27 states that the Holy Spirit is interceding on your behalf according to God's will for your life. We can be confident that God will work in His time. He is the architect of our dreams. He's orchestrating all the pieces. He will restore, and it will be so much better than if we did it ourselves.

So pray and keep praying. Ask God what He wants you to see during this time. He is our source of help. Open up your heart to Him, and ask for His help. He waits for you, and He waits for me. Isaiah 30:18–19 says, "Therefore the Lord waits to be gracious to you, and therefore he exalts himself to show mercy to you. For the Lord is a God of justice; blessed are all those who wait for him. For a people shall dwell in Zion, in Jerusalem; you shall weep no more. He will surely be gracious to you at the sound of your cry. As soon as he hears it, he answers you."

Find and ask others to help you see what you can't see.

Walk with people who can be your cheerleader and remind you of the goodness and faithfulness of God in your life. We can always find people who will sit and whine with us and come to our pity parties. It is the rare friend who can speak truth to us and remind us of what is important. Don't be too proud to reach out.

In the classes I teach at the university, many of my international students come from a cultural belief system that to ask for any help is a sign of weakness. When we talk about leaders who are facing challenges and the benefits of being authentic, it is interesting to hear their perspective. I love wrestling through the discussion and helping them come to a new paradigm shift of understanding a healthy leader will ask for help.

Remember, God can see what you can't see.

God's dream for you belongs to Him—it was never yours in the first place. You don't own it, He does. The minute you clamp your hands on it and try to claim it, it will be swept away in the storm. God's dream. God's time. God's way. God's help.

In the aftermath of my marriage's perfect storm, which led to our separation, I doubted whether God would ever allow me to write and speak again. I had doubts, and my fears threatened to overtake me. The storm leveled me so deeply and swept my self-confidence right down with it. I didn't have the resolve of those Darwin residents. *I don't think I want to live in this city anymore let alone rebuild it. I will just go live somewhere else where I don't have to be reminded of the destruction.*

I had cataclysmic doubts, and God heard my whining and grieving. I am sure it got old to His ears, and yet He is loving and faithful to gently prod me to obedience to trust Him. I started to believe the lie that my best years for serving God in a leadership ministry were behind me. I began to think the dream had reached as far as it could go, and I should just settle and be grateful.

However, as I was praying and telling God how I felt, He brought someone's name to my mind, and though I didn't hear an audible voice, I felt as though I was supposed to call her and ask her to mentor me through the gauntlet of doubt. She willingly agreed and began to pray for me and speak words of hope over what I couldn't see. She empathized but didn't allow me to wallow in my pain. She gently prodded me to believe God's promises. She didn't speak words of flattery over my gifts but words of truth. She saw what I couldn't see—God's restorative purpose in waiting. I desperately needed those life-giving words and especially her prayers. It encouraged me. It strengthened me. It inspired me to keep waiting with perseverance and listen carefully to what God was doing in my life. She helped me to remember that, just like Tabitha, I was caught somewhere between a dream and a miracle.

If you are in between a dream and a miracle right now, I believe with you and for you that God is going to complete His good work in your life. Don't give up on the dream He has entrusted to you. Don't move out of the place God has placed you just because there is a little wind and rain. God is working silently behind the scenes, and He knows, He sees, and He has a plan. Trust Him, give Him back the dream, and watch and see the miracle unfold.

Have you asked for help recently? Why or Why not?

Take some time to write out your dream and what's happened up until this point. What is the next step? Is God asking you to wait? Is He asking you to be patient? Is He asking you to call for help?

Write out a prayer, and express each emotion that is troubling you right now. Surrender it to Him in prayer.

Chapter Eight
Derecho Devastation

Nehemiah: Rebuilding Broken Teams

> Alone we can do so little. Together we can do so much.
>
> —Helen Keller, *Helen Keller: A Life*

In less than 48 hours I was due to fly to a conference, and the weather forecast for the eastern part of the United States was calling for thunderstorms. I checked with the airlines, and the customer representative on the phone commented, "Summer storms are no fun, and it could be more than bumpy." I ended the call . . . and began to work myself into a mental frenzy.

Later that night, I broke all my rules about what I do to get ready to sleep and I did some research in bed. I Googled "flying in thunderstorms." What was I thinking? It went against all my training to renew my mind and let go of toxic thoughts. My night then consisted of tossing and turning as I considered all the scenarios of bouncing up and down in the air while flying across the country. The next morning I woke up and said to God and myself, "This is utterly, ridiculously stupid! I am going to this conference, and no storm is going to stop me." My daughter-in-law Brittany, who I refer to as my daughter-in-love, rebuked me: "God is bigger than any storm, and you have to go to this event."

I arrived safely, and my two flights were uneventful. Our trip squeezed into the lull between thunderstorms, and I watched the horizon as we prepared to land as bolts of lightning flashed through the skies. I was in such awe at the power of the storm I was witnessing I forgot how afraid I'd been two nights before. It was brilliant to watch from 10,000 feet in the air. I learned the next night that it wasn't any ordinary storm; it was a low-end derecho storm.

If you haven't heard of a derecho storm, just like I hadn't, it is a series of thunderstorms that can create tornadoes. This line of storms bows out and can cause damage for at least 250 miles with well-separated wind gusts of 75 mph. Derechos cause toppled trees, power outages, flash floods, and more, and the loss can be devastating. That's exactly what happened in the span of 36 hours as I watched the news from my hotel room.

A derecho storm in life can likewise have a path that lasts more than a few days or a few weeks. It can seem to go on for a few years. When that kind of devastation occurs, everything looks hopeless, and nothing will ever be the same. That's exactly how I felt in the midst of mine and Kevin's perfect storm. It seemed to go on forever. The damage wasn't isolated to one small area, and it had a wide path. To date, it is the greatest and longest storm I've ever encountered, and for a long time, I thought it would never end.

When all seems lost and it appears that nothing will change, God breathes newness. In the rubble of devastation, hope can emerge. It takes a trained eye to see hope in the rubble. Derecho storms can crush dreams, and in leadership, they can kill teams.

In the Old Testament, Nehemiah experienced a derecho storm. To give a little background, the Jews had been held in captivity by Babylon for seventy years. As a result, Jerusalem was destroyed and lay in ruins. Nehemiah was the part of the third return of the Jewish people to Israel after their captivity. There had been seventy years of devastation held by their enemies. Hope had been crushed right out of the heart and soul of the Jewish people. They were scattered, and they didn't know who was for them or who was for God.

In all this chaos, Nehemiah served as the cupbearer under King Artaxerxes in Persia. But Nehemiah knew God and believed God. He prayed and approached the king to ask if he could rebuild what was lost, what was forgotten, what was destroyed. He saw the ruins of his beloved city and wept. The king agreed Nehemiah could go to Jerusalem. He knew he couldn't do it alone, so Nehemiah built a team. The Jews were scattered, and he was aware that a team of rescuers who would rally together could turn broken dreams into new life and new hope. The city wasn't the only thing that needed to be rebuilt. The people also needed restoration. They too had broken dreams.

The Book of Nehemiah gives us the answers on how to leverage a team after a derecho-type storm.

There are many scenarios that can catapult a team into a storm-like situation, even an unintended storm of a natural sequence of events. In the context of church ministry and organizations, teams can disband when there is a turnover of new leadership. Long-term staff leaving can suddenly change team dynamics. When a senior leader changes course or makes unwise decisions either professionally or personally, it can cause distrust in a team as they watch their leader falter. Change in culture whether by default or conflict of shared values can bring tension and disunity to a team if not handled well. These and other scenarios can create the need to either rebuild a team or redefine the team from the ground up.

Many leaders find themselves ill equipped to handle the change, and without the right kind of support it can put a team back a hundred steps and hurt the organization significantly.

There are some excellent books on building effective teams. I have the privilege of teaching both adult learners and international students in the leadership program at Trinity Western University. I love using Patrick Lencioni's materials in class and as a leader on more than one occasion when I am looking to move a team forward or to strengthen an existing team. In his book, *The Advantage*, he asserts, "Teamwork is not a virtue. It is a choice—and a strategic one."

If this is true, then effective team building is critical to accomplishing God's purposes. We aren't meant to be influencers and leaders alone. We are created for community and to work together on every level of life. In Henry Cloud's book, *The Power of the Other*, he shares how our relationships are dynamically synced to our productivity and performance, and there is a science involved in the connecting of relationships, whether right or bad, and our ability to succeed. We need each other in every season, and it is critical to moving forward, especially when we encounter storms and are giving it our best to recover.

And yet there is a lot we can learn from the story of Nehemiah as it represents a progression of steps, which happened to rebuild the wall in Jerusalem. Let's take a peek into Nehemiah's strategy and how God used him to rally the troops among the rubble and ruin.

Prayer and Passion

First of all, we see Nehemiah's heart is rooted in prayer and desire. From the initial vision of the walls being rebuilt to the reconstruction and dedication, Nehemiah uses prayer. He is dedicated to honoring and glorifying God in the whole process.

In Nehemiah 1, Nehemiah meets with a group of men who had just come from Jerusalem. His inquiry of his beloved city and the reports of destruction drove him to his knees, "When I heard these things, I sat down and wept. For some days I mourned and fasted and prayed before the God of heaven" (v. 4 NIV).

Nehemiah's prayer, a prayer of humility and great passion for his people, births a God-sized vision. The city of Jerusalem can be rebuilt and restored to its former state of protection for God's chosen people, the Jews. But Nehemiah's cry goes beyond mere physical walls; it calls for a return and revival to the Lord in obedience.

I admire Nehemiah's motivation to pray. It comes from his passion for God's people and the city he loves. I have to admit I am not a very good "pray-er." I love to study God's Word and read, but I have to discipline myself to pray. My natural instinct is to fix what's wrong immediately without even a wisp of a prayer. This isn't God's way of taking the first step. But Nehemiah's passion for God and His people is what propelled Nehemiah to actively pray first rather than start into action.

When we find our way out of a storm and take a moment to look around at the devastation, it's hard to feel passion, much less a desire to pray. It feels overwhelming. It can be easier to cling to fragile emotions rather than trust God and pray. We come to the realization that we can't stay in this place; we have to move forward, and to pray is the first step!

That's where our will comes in, so that we can make a conscious decision to stand up in the ruins and be determined to not stay in one place. As we pray, our thinking shifts so that new ideas form. As we call on God to mold and heal us, we develop ideas needed to recruit a team or how to restructure an already existing team. I can't tell you how many times when I have disciplined myself to pray, God has rewarded my effort to consult Him first. He has many times brought specific names to mind or surprised me with a conversation I hadn't intended when I am structuring a team for a project. As I step back and commit to pray, I see my human wisdom for what it is— small in comparison to God's wisdom.

I believe a split second moment in prayer is when our passion is awakened, and we begin to actively lean in and pray with fervor. In prayer, God often reveals the bigger picture when all seems in ruins. In our conversation with God, we gain His perspective.

We gain a supernatural God-confidence to dust ourselves off, and we start looking up instead of focusing on the rubble. By looking up we find His direction, and we have a part in getting there, even in the midst of difficulty and hardship. Praying for renewal bolsters not just you as the leader, but it also energizes the team. Corporate prayer brings people together like nothing else can. It is natural to want to begin strategizing instead of committing to pray, but the foundation to bringing a team back into focus is learning to pray together.

If you have been in leadership for anytime, what I've said probably isn't new. It isn't profound, and yet it is a simple truth that can sometimes be easy to skip over.

Ruth Haley Barton, in her book, *Pursuing God's Will Together*, shares how she consults with leaders on finding discernment corporately, "Leaders are often a bit surprised when I tell them where we need to begin. They usually have the idea that there is some sort of technique I can teach in a weekend that will send them off and running. But what I tell them is that corporate discernment begins with attending to the spiritual formation of each individual leader." She follows up with helping leaders in their spiritual practices such as solitude and silence so they can know how to listen to God. She goes on to make a critical point, "Solitude is the foundational discipline of the spiritual life; it is time set aside to give God our full and undivided attention."

This is what we see in Nehemiah's life—he slows down, prays, gives God his full attention, and consults God about how to proceed.

Even when there is passion and prayer, moving forward isn't necessarily crystal clear. As we choose to hunker down in prayer—and I might add asking others to join us—clarity brings focus. The focus cements the vision, and God brings other people around to guide us.

Waiting . . . and More Waiting

According to the Jewish calendar, it was about four months after Nehemiah prayed his prayer before the king took notice of Nehemiah's grief and gave Nehemiah permission to return to Jerusalem. I find God's timing in answering Nehemiah sobering. Often, a birth of vision comes from passion and prayer, and in our human nature we think it must transpire immediately. We should get the team going *now!* Let's get those walls rebuilt! Let's get this team moving! Let's institute this new program because it will breathe new life into the wreckage of the storm. This isn't necessarily God's way.

When my marriage was in crisis, in an attempt to lessen any of our issues spilling over into the church, we tried to rebuild and move ahead too quickly. The church lovingly sent us off for intense counseling, but several decades of dysfunction was not going to be repaired in a three-month period. We were unable to keep our problems from naturally spilling over into the church leadership and beyond. There was a vast chasm, and moving ahead prematurely only proved to cause more distrust in the team and congregation. Trust had to be rebuilt.

Even though they were empathetic to our marriage crisis and our struggle, it still impacted the very core of our staff. I best describe it as being admitted to the intensive care unit of a hospital and making a decision to leave against medical advice. We didn't allow enough time for wounds to heal, and the consequences spread like a contagion. We made mistakes, and many people were hurt. Gratefully, God has overwhelmingly shown mercy through forgiveness and healing. I don't understand everything, but I believe God knows the bigger picture. As Kevin and I look back, we see God's grace displayed through the church in allowing us the room and space to continue to work out our issues.

That's why timing is crucial in restoring after a storm. It isn't an easy fix. There are no boxes to tick off. It takes lots of solitude, silence, praying, fasting, counseling, and crying out before God, and this is what we see in Nehemiah.

In Nehemiah's situation, I have to believe in what we imagine happened during the four-month gap between chapters one and two—Nehemiah as he continued to pray for God's wisdom and the right timing to approach the pagan king with his request. He took a significant risk but, girded and grounded in prayer, God paved the way for his success.

I get impatient at times when God reveals a vision; I get restless when I don't see restoration happen. I want it to happen now, especially if I am picking myself up out of the mud. But something happens when I choose to wait. The picture gets clearer, and God brings others alongside who can affirm that waiting is good. Waiting is healthy, and waiting is God's way of getting me to let go of what I think should take place.

Rally for Restoration

After all the praying and waiting and leaning in, it was time for Nehemiah to rally his team. It was time for him to pull out all the passion he could muster and cast the vision to see who would join the team to rebuild the wall.

Nehemiah gave a terse account to the city officials and religious leaders.

> "Face it: we're in a bad way here. Jerusalem is a wreck; its gates are burned up. Come—let's build the wall of Jerusalem and not live with this disgrace any longer." I told them how God was supporting me and how the king was backing me up.
>
> —Nehemiah 2:17–18 *The Message*

In his book *Courageous Leadership*, Bill Hybels affirms Nehemiah's plight, "When God gives you a vision you'll know it. You'll see it clearly and feel it deeply." Nehemiah cast the vision with passion by presenting the problem as something that affected everyone, and if they worked together, they could make a difference. He identified the need by appealing to them emotionally in regard to their heritage as Jews and the importance of the city of Jerusalem to the foundation of their culture for centuries. He appealed to their broken souls. He pleaded with them they couldn't stay where they were. They had to do something! I would surmise if we had the full text of his message we would see he delivered it with great enthusiasm and conviction. Nehemiah evidently succeeded because the people stated, "'We're with you. Let's get started.' They rolled up their sleeves, ready for the good work" (v. 18 *The Message*). Not one of them wanted their city to be disgraced, except for a few non-Jew officials who felt threatened by the Jews' success. Nehemiah led the people from where they were to where they needed to go and enlisted those who shared his passion.

Brokenness can do that. It can rally a team. A vision for restoration can bring a group together like nothing else can. It puts everyone on the same playing field because everyone is suffering in some way. All the years the Jews had suffered in exile, they felt displaced and longed for home.

The ongoing refugee crisis in our world reflects the need for restoration. We have watched and read about hundreds and thousands of refugees in the past year looking for a place they can call home. They are much like the Jews who were scattered and forced into exile. They need a place to rebuild their lives, a place to restore, a place to feel safe and, much like in Nehemiah's time, a place to bring healing restoration to their souls.

In Nehemiah 3, we see the nitty-gritty of a turnaround. The team is mobilized effectively and is equipped to do the work of repairing the walls around Jerusalem. Great detail is given with attention to the names of the workers and the portion of the walls they repaired.

According to Gene Wilkes in his book, *Jesus on Leadership*, building an effective team involves these four steps: "Create a sense of togetherness; empower with authority and presence; account for the mission and the team's actions; and be a mentor."

As the Jews work to rebuild the walls around Jerusalem, you find a strong sense of togetherness and get the impression of them working side by side. We see strong leadership in their oversight of the project. Specifics are given as to what and how the gates and walls are to be repaired. Because we don't hear of Nehemiah in this chapter, we can gather he was giving oversight to the team leaders and mentoring them in the success of rebuilding. We don't see an ego-controlling leader, but rather we hear of how each area is functioning to accomplish the goal. We see harmony and unity in the project among the workers. They are connected and serving in unity.

A team works when each team member catches the vision. Each team member is confident and secure with their contribution of their worth of gifting and abilities. Each team member sees his or her strengths as a part of the puzzle to the grander picture. The team members begin to work in harmony and sync with each other. They move as one toward a common goal and start to build momentum toward restoration. Their leader fuels the team with empowerment.

Perseverance and Grit

Like any restoration project, there are setbacks. We shouldn't be surprised by setbacks. When we are building God's kingdom, the enemy wants to put stumbling blocks in our way so we will feel defeated and give up. And in Nehemiah 4—6 the opposition mounts. Rumors begin to circulate.

> Sanballat was very angry when he learned that we were rebuilding the wall. He flew into a rage and mocked the Jews, saying in front of his friends and the Samarian army officers, "What does this bunch of poor, feeble Jews think they're doing? Do they think they can build the wall in a single day by just offering a few sacrifices? Do they actually think they can make something of stones from a rubbish heap—and charred ones at that?"
>
> —Nehemiah 4:1–2 NLT

Discouragement started to set in, and Nehemiah did what he knew best—he prayed. He prayed for strength and courage to persevere in the midst of opposition. He assembled the leaders and the people and gave them words of courage and reminded them God Almighty was fighting for them. The people returned to work—this time with guards and weapons, fully prepared for enemy attack.

When God gives a vision and momentum is building, often the enemy moves in to taunt, attack, and discourage for one purpose—so we will give up! He wants to send us back to remembering the ruin of the storm and for us to set up camp there. He wants us to sit in the rubble and settle down right there so we never reach our potential. When the wall is half built, he wants us to quit the team. How many of us have stopped just short of success without realizing it? How many times have you and I settled for a half-built wall in our lives?

In her book, *Grit: The Power of Passion and Perseverance*, Angela Duckworth presents a grit scale she developed while studying the success of students at the United States Military Academy at West Point. The ten-question scale is intended to determine just how gritty a person is and has a series of questions aimed at identifying two components in life—passion and perseverance. Duckworth asserts the two are linked in determining success and not necessarily based on how smart a person is. She says, "Grit is about working on something you care about so much that you're willing to stay loyal to it." And, I might add, no matter the challenge!

In spite of the obstacles, Nehemiah led the people to persevere, and their passion is what drove them not to give up. The roadblocks caused them to work smarter, "And each of the builders had his sword strapped at his side while he built" (v. 18). They implemented a practical way to persevere and be committed to the project, giving them confidence as they worked.

Persevering, for us, means activating our spiritual weapons listed in Ephesians 6, taking up our shield of faith and our sword of the Spirit, putting on the full armor of God every single day and taking on the stature of a warrior in battle. This is godly grit. The fire in our passion for finishing what God has called us to enables us to persevere and overcome the challenges.

Recently, I was wrestling through some tough choices and was feeling discouraged. Isaiah 50:7 (NIV) reminded me, "Because the Sovereign LORD helps me, I will not be disgraced. Therefore, I have set my face like flint, and I know I will not be put to shame." The verse is written on a card for me to look at and live boldly with determination to take the steps of obedience in what God is asking me to do.

How do we endure amidst the attack? Stay focused. In other words, remember your purpose, the big picture, and why you can't stay where you once were. This is grit—staying loyal to the commitment and the team. The opposition and struggles are minor compared to the rewards of seeing the end results. This is what Nehemiah was communicating to the people—don't give up, and don't quit; God is with us and will fight for us because this is His dream too!

Too often the enthusiasm of a vision and dream wears off when we encounter resistance. It is then our passion ignites, and perseverance is applied for the accomplishment of the goal. Godly endurance is practicing grit for the health of the team and the mission. I believe that during a time of conflict some of the greatest work of team building takes places while in the nitty-gritty challenge of the project. Let's be people of grit!

Promise of Renewal

The rest of the Book of Nehemiah is a brilliant account of revival in the hearts of the Jews in Jerusalem. I am sure Nehemiah didn't have a clue of how far reaching the initial vision with the team he built was. His beloved city is restored, but far greater the people responded in humble worship and adoration of God. Nehemiah 9 is an excellent picture of true worship as a result of the restoration of a team for greater good. The description of their spiritual renewal challenges me in my pursuit of intimacy with God. The vision is fulfilled, and authentic revival takes place.

> They remained standing in place for three hours while the Book of the Law of the Lord their God was read aloud to them. Then for three more hours they confessed their sins and worshiped the Lord their God. The Levites . . . stood on the stairway of the Levites and cried out to the Lord their God with loud voices.
>
> —Nehemiah 9:3–4 NLT

Rebuilding a team after a storm takes plenty of passion, continuous prayer, waiting, and more waiting, rallying to restoration, perseverance, and grit to see the promise and fulfillment of recovery. A team proves the most basic human need; we can't live or work without each other. To "do life" we need to rely on each other.

It takes a lot to come back after a derecho storm, and Nehemiah leads the way with his example of perseverance and courage.

Is your team facing any obstacles? How will you attack the challenge?

Where in your life do you need to become grittier to stay committed to your calling?

Chapter Nine

Haboob Havoc

David: When You Doubt

Our doubts are traitors and make us lose the good
we oft might win by fearing to attempt.

—William Shakespeare, *Measure for Measure*

Haboob is an unusual name for a storm, don't you think?
Usually, *haboobs* happen in the Sahara and the Arabian
Peninsula. In North America, they can be found in Arizona, California, and Texas. A *haboob* is a dust storm,
but not a regular dust storm. Dr. Thomas Gill, an associate professor and graduate advisor of the Department of
Geological Sciences at the University of Texas, El Paso,
defines a *haboob* as "A giant wall or front of dust that
blows in often to a clear, calm sky. Sometimes, it comes
out of nowhere."

This type of storm can be as much as 60 miles wide
and throw winds from about 20 to 60 mph and higher. It
creates blizzard-like whiteout conditions with the particles of dust and debris that is lifted up in the air. They
appear ominous and threatening. *Haboobs* are the vigorous gusts of dust that ride out in front of a thunderstorm.
In 2011 in Phoenix, Arizona, an almost mile-high wall of
dust knocked out power lines and stopped airline flights,
coating everything in its path with thick dust.

I can't even imagine being in a storm like a *haboob*. We often visit family in Palm Desert, California, and we have been caught a time or two in a sand storm. Everything sticks to you. The sand gets in your eyes, attaches to your scalp, and deposits grit between your teeth, not to mention annoying little spaces in your clothes and shoes. We run for cover when we see one coming, but even in the safety of the house, I am always amazed at just how much sand sneaks in.

When David was fleeing from Saul, he was caught in a type of *haboob*. Saul was bent on crushing David. His insecurities about David were exacerbated, and he felt threatened because of Samuel's anointing of David as the next king of Israel. In 1 Samuel 27 we find David feeling a little weary and worried that Saul was going to catch up with him. He says in his heart, "Now I shall perish one day by the hand of Saul. There is nothing better for me than that I should escape to the land of the Philistines" (v. 1).

Is this the same faith-filled David who fought the giant Goliath ten chapters earlier? Even though he was next in line for the throne and had seen the mighty hand of God in his life, his weariness and doubt caught up with him. He found himself living in the midst of the Philistines who had given him refuge in exchange for help defeating their mutual enemies.

David decided to ask for a place to retreat with his men and families instead of living in the royal city. Achish, the Philistine son of the king of Gath, gave him Ziklag. This town was away from the crowded capital, and they could have more freedom to live in the way they were used to. Ziklag became the refuge for David, his men, and their families for the sixteen months they lived in the region of their enemies. The rest of the chapter relates how David and his men went out day after day fighting the battles. The threat of the storm seemed ominous, and I am sure David wondered when it would hit in full force. Was the dust swirling around his mind clouding his vision? David has been fighting for some time, and some of his victories might be seen as small dust storms that were easily defeated. The combination of Saul relentlessly chasing him and the unrest in his heart caused his doubt to grow, and you can see how it develops into a *haboob*-type storm.

Before a *haboob* hits, you can see it in the distance. As the wind moves closer, you lose visibility because everything is stirred up by the powerful winds. We might think of the winds in a personal *haboob* as stirring up doubts in our mind because of what we believe we see in the distance. In this case, David saw the storm of Saul chasing him and the feeling of being displaced and living among people who didn't share the same values and the same Jehovah God.

Every leader has doubts. It's normal. All of us can find ourselves in positions of questioning our leadership, whether we lead a small group, are a senior leader of an organization, or somewhere in between. If you don't have any doubts, then I would suggest something is wrong. Small dust storms seem manageable. But day after day, week after week, they build into larger storms like a *haboob*. It gets wearisome and feels threatening. Like David, battle weary, we walk out our doors each day suited up in our armor and face head on whatever the day brings. Will we ever get a break? It's during these times the enemy whispers those swirling particles of doubts to us as he did to David. And we speak into our hearts all the fears of trying to figure out how to keep our confidence alive day by day.

There are seasons when it seems as though we can't seem to catch our breath. Each day feels like a major battle. That's the time when everything we've trained for is tested. Everything we learn in our spiritual boot camp gets put into action. We find out what we are made of and how much we trust God to help us fight our battles. It has been said you learn what a leader is made of when their character is tested in a time of adversity.

Leadership isn't for wimps. It is down and dirty and plain ol' hard some days. We can be flying high seeing God's favor and success and the next we are fighting enemies that seem to come out of the woodwork. Life wears on us and the demands press in and creates ruts of despair in our spirit. If we aren't careful, those ruts become permanent, and we lose the ground we are battling. How do we stand strong when we are in a Ziklag situation? When we feel displaced and all we seem to do is fight in a bloody war? How can we prepare to stand firm when looming dust clouds threaten to fog our perspective and cause unnecessary doubt?

I know one place and one place only of how to conquer the doubts and suit up for the battle—God's Word. No, this isn't a new or profound concept. But it's the truth. Serving on the front lines, we must have an ironclad strategy—a God strategy. We have to be discerning as David was waiting to be crowned king. He was already anointed. He was simply living in a temporary residence before he ascended to the throne.

In many ways, we are like David. We are waiting as we battle for the promised future. No, we won't be crowned king or queen, but we waiting for the promise of being reunited with our King, Jesus Christ, the one and only true King. We are like David living in Ziklag, a place that isn't our real home. This home is temporary before we go to the place God has promised He has prepared for us.

> Let not your hearts be troubled. Believe in God; believe also in me. In my Father's house are many rooms. If it were not so, would I have told you that I go to prepare a place for you? And if I go and prepare a place for you, I will come again and will take you to myself, that where I am you may be also.
>
> —John 14:1–3

Jesus is telling us to wait, hold on, and not be troubled; He has gone ahead to get things ready for us. As I am working on this chapter, my ninety-six-year-old mother-in-love is standing at the doors of heaven getting ready to enter the rooms God has prepared for her. She fought the good fight, she won her struggle, and victory is now here, and we are grateful. She left her temporary home of Ziklag and has entered the promised rest.

That is our hope as we are weary, doubtful, and troubled. God has gone ahead of us to get things ready. Our job is to continue to stand strong in whatever situation we find ourselves in and doing battle in the small things day after day. Being faithful in the drudgery sometimes, it's not the huge issues that send us over the edge as leaders, it's the little dust storms that swirl around us each day, which lead to the obstacles we fight. Being a warrior isn't for the faint of heart. It takes an effort to get up sore and bruised and put on the armor every single day. Satan wants us to get lost in the small skirmishes and forget about the big picture. Don't be tempted to go there and give your energy to the things that don't matter in the long run.

I've made it a habit lately to get up in the morning and read Ephesians 6:10–18. Some days I miss, but I realize the only way to survive living in Ziklag is to consciously put on my spiritual armor daily. Paul starts by saying, "Finally, be strong in the Lord and in the strength of his might" (v. 10). When I speak that out loud, it makes me take notice. It isn't about me! I don't have to do it all by myself. That's the rut I referred to earlier, and the rut tricks us into thinking we have to figure it all out by ourselves and hide away in Ziklag as David was doing.

God says otherwise. How do we live in Ziklag as a warrior fighting the battle? There are two principles driving me to keep in the fight and not be enticed by the *haboob* I see in the distance.

First, be strong in the strength of His might. I can be immovable in His power, His strength, His competence, His command, His control. Another word I found for *knowledge* and *competence* is *moxie*. I can be immovable in God's moxie! Are you weary? Where are your doubts? Be strong in God's might. A trained warrior knows his strength can't come just from himself. It has to originate from an outside source. And in our case, God the Mighty King is mighty to save. The pressure is off to be strong in ourselves. We can live in Ziklag and be strong.

Second, don't give up. "And let us not grow weary of doing good, for in due season we will reap, if we do not give up" (Galatians 6:9). There have been many times in my calling I have been tempted to give up. But it is my passion for Jesus that keeps me standing in my armor bloodied and weary believing the truth of Galatians. We can't give up. There is too much at stake. As leaders, people are watching, and people need someone they can count on. Let me say it again; we can't give up! Know yourself well enough to not follow the train of thought that takes you down the path of giving up. When I am tired and overwhelmed, I am tempted to give up. I know that about myself. So I go to bed. I take a nap. I take a walk. I indulge in something fun to remind me that life is good. I've learned the weak points in my armor and what to do.

It's been said you find out what a person is made of when they are tested. You discover what kind of character they have when they are pushed against the wall. We will be tested; we will get sand in our teeth and dust in our eyes. It's what we do in those moments in the battle like David that will determine our success.

David's *haboob* descended on him down the road, as is outlined in the Book of 1 Samuel. Because David was an ally with the Philistines, he is caught in a position to fight with them against Saul and Israel. The Philistines decided it would be a conflict of interest, and they requested he and his men not fight and rather go back to Ziklag. When they came to their home three days later, they found their enemies the Amalekites had raided their town, burned it to the ground, and took their wives and children as captives. This was the worst day of his life. David and his loyal men wept uncontrollably it says, "Until they had no more strength to weep" (1 Samuel 30:4). They cried the deep guttural cries of hopelessness for they had been decimated. David was deeply distressed as the story goes, and his men turned on him and wanted to kill him. They had been fighting long and hard, and this suffering was too great to bear. David found himself alone.

But David didn't give up. He didn't let his meltdown dictate his actions. He got off his knees, dried his tears with the back of his hand, and Scripture says he "Strengthened himself in the LORD his God" (v. 6). He persisted and bound himself to God where he knew from previous experience God would come through. Even when his men rejected him, he was aware that God is faithful. He had a history of God's faithfulness in his life, and that is no different from you or me.

In the crucial confrontation of the storm when the sand and debris threaten to obscure God's outrageous grace, we need to strengthen ourselves in God. Seek God in your weakness, just as David did following the cry fest. He asked God if he should we go after his enemies. God gave David the signal that He was with them and David's mission would rescue and restore what was lost. The story ends with, "David recovered all that the Amalekites had taken, and David rescued his two wives. Nothing was missing, whether small or great, sons or daughters, spoil or anything that had been taken. David brought back all" (vv. 18–19). His knee-jerk reaction revealed his character, and whether his men stood with him or not, his leadership intuition told him he could rely on God.

We are living in perilous times. We certainly can agree on that. The days are confusing now more than ever. We are called to stand strong in our identity in Jesus no matter what *haboob* cloud looms in the distance to threaten destruction. Don't give up, don't give in, and strengthen yourself in who you know God to be in your life. He promises to come through even if a lot of sand gets in your teeth. You will be victorious!

Make a list of times in your life when you have seen the faithfulness of God come through in a storm.

Write out a prayer thanking God for how He has rescued you.

Decide what piece of armor needs to be strengthened to encourage you to keep going strong in the Lord.

Chapter Ten

CYCLONES OF UNCERTAINTY

Priscilla and Aquila: Trusting in the Unknown

There will be very few occasions when you are absolutely certain about anything. You will consistently be called upon to make decisions with limited information. That being the case, your goal should not be to eliminate uncertainty. Instead, you must develop the art of being clear in the face of uncertainty.

—Andy Stanley, *Next Generation Leader*

One of the things I love about being a life coach is helping people clarify their purpose and find their stride. Most of us, if not all of us, find several times throughout our lives of living in uncertainty. Change can be disconcerting and even frightening. But instead of dreading change we can see it as a window of time that provides a chance to see the broader landscape. It is often in these moments God moves us further onto His agenda.

When life is sure, the temptation is to get too comfortable. We are creatures of habit, and we like our routines. It works after all, so why break the cycle? Living wholly surrendered to God means our lives are not our own. We give the Creator of the universe permission to mix things up and move things around even if it means taking us out of our comfort zones. The undoing of a leader is thinking uncertainty is the enemy. Rather I find uncertainty is a God opportunity to help shift us to the next level of leadership and more accurately into the next level of character He is building in us.

Living in uncertainty can be like watching a cyclone off in the distance. We see those winds circling and wonder how they will impact us. We aren't sure how and where the storm will hit. It is in the waiting with God where we find peace in the eye and center of the storm.

When I work with leaders who are facing transition I often take them through a basic process on purpose. Why? Because it is good to revisit who we are and where we see God in our lives and assess our experiences and abilities. I call it the "What do I know to be true about me?" exercise. I help them evaluate their values, strengths, and weaknesses and create or revisit their mission statement. Staying true to who you know you are in Jesus helps you not fear the uncertainty of the winds even if they are within striking distance and feel too close for comfort.

There are things that happen as a result of uncertainty. Sometimes we doubt our calling. We question whether or not we heard God right. We wrestle. We ask questions. We flip back and forth analyzing our life and experiences. Is that a bad thing? I don't think so. Thinking critically in a time of uncertainty and using discernment is wisdom. If you find yourself in a place of uncertainty, ask the hard questions. Why am I doing what I am doing? Have I experienced any defining moments of affirmation along the way? Am I focused on my primary gifts for maximum impact? Ask others around you; find people in your life who will let you ask the hard questions and not just tell you what you want to hear.

Other times we see uncertainty as the end of something we thought was good. But change or the end of one assignment doesn't necessarily mean there is not goodness ahead. Remember, God is good all of the time, not only when things are going well, ministry is soaring, and you see incredible results. God is good in the valleys. God is good in the crisis. God is good in the uncertainty . . . all of the time.

I challenge you to think of uncertainty as an opportunity to bring closure to a chapter in a book while anticipating a new chapter ahead. God is the one writing your story, and he often writes our story in chapters. There is, however, a measure of mystery, as Paul David Tripp writes in his book, *New Morning Mercies*, "There will always be a mystery in your life. God will always surprise you with what he brings your way. You will always be confronted with the unplanned and the unexpected. All of this is because you don't rule your life and you don't write your own story."

Sometimes transitions naturally occur in our leadership and others come as a result of a storm. When shifts usually happen, they can be seamless, and the measure of uncertainty can be minimal. However, when it is as a result of a storm it can shake us up, and we can question everything about our leadership and our calling. This is a good thing. Standing strong in a storm of uncertainty brings a larger sense of clarity in ways that otherwise wouldn't have come.

We think that living in the in-between is a waste of time, and time is short! This is the biggest lie on the planet. The waiting in the middle of what was and what will be is some of the most significant times in our lives. It is in these times of waiting that God does His best work in our lives. What we might think is a waste is where the dream is refined, and our character reemerges with grace we didn't have before. In his book, *The In-Between: Embracing the Tension Between Now and the Next Best Thing*, Jeff

Goins says, "In the in-between we learn to recognize the temporal nature of life, and that eventually all waiting must end. When it does, we are left with what we did with the time in between the beginning and the end."

The in-between times are some of the most eye-opening seasons, and if I did not walk through the tension of those times, I wouldn't be where I am today as a person and as a leader. Embracing the in-between times helps us to stand strong in times of uncertainty.

Cara Meredith, in an article for *Christianity Today*, writes how Rianna Shaw Robinson, minister of city engagement at Oakland City Church, recalls a time when discomfort helped her clarify her calling. Rianna found herself in the in-between before serving on the staff of OCC. She had left her familiar, safe church of her African American heritage and started attending the multiethnic community of OCC. She struggled in this new multiethnic environment, and she stated that the multiethnic church model initially "felt like an attack on a place that for so many oppressed people was a place of refuge." The lead pastor encouraged her to do something about it, and she began working through Donald Miller's book *Storyline* with a group of women, discovering the thread of how God was working in her life and redeeming her for His purpose.

As she continued to look for clarity by asking some hard questions, getting involved at OCC, and becoming a lay leader, things began to fall into place, and her vision became clearer. After two years, Rianna made a decision to continue her education and began working at OCC. Although she works hard to juggle her family, pursuit of education, and ministry, she believes God has called her to be a relationship bridge builder when it comes to issues of social action and race. She's learned, "I've accepted that I will likely find myself in situations where I don't feel 100 percent comfortable. But I know that God is using me toward the restoration of everyone who has been impacted by systems of oppression and white supremacy. And that means everyone: the oppressed and the oppressors, the victims and the beneficiaries."

Waiting and living in the in-between is the place God defines and redeems our awkward moments. There are a few things we can learn from Rianna's story; first of all, she didn't sit on her hands when she came to a place of struggle in the in-between. Rianna continued to serve for two years as a lay leader. That might not have been her first choice, but she continued to be proactive as she sought God's guidance. There is always movement in waiting if you look closely. In the movement of her waiting, clarity began to come full circle for her as she served.

Secondly, she came to the conclusion she was not always going to be 100 percent comfortable. It is important to be OK living in the rhythm of the in-between moments. Embracing the tension of the uncertainty helps us trust God in a deeper way than we have before. How fervently we embrace the waiting reveals what we believe about God and how much we trust Him to work behind the scenes orchestrate the pieces of our lives. It's not easy, but it is necessary.

Those periods of waiting and living in the in-between can seem like an eternity, and we can wonder what God is up to. Our whole calling shifts in some way. But our vision illuminates in this tension. Our passion burns stronger. Our faith increases as we see how the puzzle pieces all fit together in the in-between. Don't despise the in-between when you face swirling winds of a cyclone. Stay close to the eye of the storm, and that tension you live in will bring clarity of what God has for you in the rebuilding and refining.

Priscilla and Aquila's testimony marks a similar pressure if you look behind the curtain of their story. In Acts 18:1–4,

Paul meets them for the first time as he arrives in Corinth on his second missionary journey:

> After this Paul left Athens and went to Corinth. And he found a Jew named Aquila, a native of Pontus, recently come from Italy with his wife Priscilla, because Claudius had commanded all the Jews to leave Rome. And he went to see them, and because he was of the same trade he stayed with them and worked, for they were tentmakers by trade.

The emperor of Rome decided to oust all the Christians, and Priscilla and Aquila found themselves in a new place, Corinth, and probably feeling a little uncertain. The Bible doesn't say why they decided to settle in that particular city. Corinth was a hub for trade and travel and yet was known all over the Roman Empire for its reputation of scandal and wickedness. It was a sordid place. Maybe the couple determined to settle there because it was good for their trade and could provide a way to minister along their vocation. It wasn't the easiest place to start over and plant a church.

The tension of their in-between time of waiting for clarity may have been from the time they left Rome to arriving in Corinth and meeting Paul. We don't know for certain, but we do know this couple was a significant part of Paul's ministry. They traveled with him to Ephesus and were instrumental in teaching Apollo, an Alexandrian disciple who was well educated and "competent in the Scriptures" (v. 24) who boldly taught in the synagogues but didn't have a full understanding of Jesus and the way of Christianity. Priscilla and Aquila helped to disciple him. Later Paul gives greetings to the Corinthians from Priscilla and Aquila, who he says have a church in their home (1 Corinthians 16:19).

Between leaving Rome and starting over in Corinth, there may have been a season of waiting, the in-between, and uncertainty. But again, we can speculate the outcome of their ministry was because of their continued movement. God was working behind the scenes, and the encounter with Paul turned into a significant relationship with the overall mission of the gospel.

The mystery of uncertainty is that the uncertainty doesn't always have to be uncertain. I know that sounds like an oxymoron, but following and listening to God's voice in the unknown can become unclouded when we believe He knows what He is doing. My friend and ministry partner, Vicki, recently experienced this certain uncertainty. We have served together for nearly two decades. We didn't formally serve together on our church staff but worked side by side with colleagues on various projects we were both passionate about.

Each year, Vicki chooses a word she believes will help her focus for the year, and in 2015 her word was *finish*. She told me, "With the two most important women in my life leaving me [her mother's passing and her daughter getting married and moving out of state] I thought perhaps *finish* meant certain key relationships. Never once did I think it had anything to do with me vocationally."

Vicki found herself feeling restless with a sense of little to no fulfillment. In her words, "I prayed earnestly asking for an understanding of what was going on inside me but didn't receive clarity on anything." She even had two people approach her, sensing they had a word of encouragement from God for her. That brought some measure of reassurance so she could continue in her ministry. You might call this the beginning of her in-between time.

As she continued in her role on the staff at our church, she came to the conclusion that she was supposed to resign. Her time was up. But she didn't know what was around the corner. That didn't stump Vicki at all because she is a woman of deep faith and trust. The word *finish* was complete in more ways than she imagined, and yet she sensed God reassigning her. Vicki is still living in the in-between, but the clarity is coming. Vicki is still serving and being proactive listening for God's voice. There is movement in the waiting, and I believe it will come for her.

That's the mystery of uncertainty. We don't always know the exact timing of when the in-between time is going to end. But we are aware it will. We just keep doing what God asks us to do. He is in control of the swirling winds—how strong, how long, and how wide a path they will travel. He is the only one who stops the swirling winds of uncertainty, and our assignment is for us to stay tucked next to Jesus in the eye of the storm as close as we can so we know what to do next.

If you are in a place of uncertainty, what bothers you most about it? Write down the things you need from God to keep close and assured.

Make a note of when you think the in-between time began.

What do you sense God is saying to you in the waiting?

Chapter Eleven
FLOOD FAITH

Levites and Priests: Leading in Faith

The task of a leader is to get his people from where they are to where they have not been.

—Henry Kissinger

Jenna was admitted to the hospital when she was only twenty-two weeks pregnant. When her water broke at nineteen weeks, she and her husband Koby began their long journey of having their faith tested.

Koby and Jenna are in full-time ministry in the greater Vancouver area of British Columbia, Canada. They have an intense fervor to raise up the next generation for Jesus. Their leadership passion is contagious, and they aren't afraid of a challenge. But little did they know the storm and floods they were about to step into would seek to overwhelm them.

Little Judah was born when Jenna was twenty-five weeks pregnant. He weighed 1 lb. 14 oz. and was considered a micro preemie. From the start, there were multiple complications with his lungs and brain. Koby and Jenna clung to the only truth that could sustain them in the floodwaters, and it was their faith in Jesus.

Four weeks into their journey she wrote on her blog after a particularly tough day:

When I left the room in the intense moment, I have to tell you, the faith that rose up in me was pretty awesome—not because of me, but because of Jesus' strength in me. I began to pray for my son to have *life* and *hope*, out loud for all to hear . . . Crazy Christian Mom strikes again! That Lioness-mama was digging her claws in. So on the day that felt like the best day ever, we also almost lost him. The emotions and the ups and downs we are experiencing are sometimes so hard—feel so heavy to bear. I'm also learning that the grace we have been given is *so* real. We have strength for each moment—the good and the bad—because our God is so good and so present. One of the nurses even came and prayed with me!

I have followed Jenna and Koby's journey with little Judah and their family since he was born. I have been in awe that despite challenge after challenge, they have remained steadfast. I am certain they have their meltdown moments, but the witness of their faith and trust in God in every situation soars above and marks the miracle of their story.

When God calls us out into deep waters, He promises to give us exactly what we need. Jenna and Koby choose to confess it loud and clear. We know the truth as God's children, we teach it as leaders, and yet do we fathom the depth of what it truly means? Do we live it out, boldly proclaiming that we believe God is in the storm? Forgive me if I sound overly spiritual or not very profound, but it is the simple truth of what our faith is all about. And yes, it is that simple. He knows we are like little children who need to hear it over and over again until it sinks in. It is as straightforward as making a choice of what we are going to think about. What we think about is what we believe. What we believe is what we will act on. And what we act on is how we respond to the storm.

I am going to take us to a familiar story in the Book of Joshua. Maybe you've preached, taught, or memorized this faith principle, but it is still a good reminder. I love that God's Word is timeless; it never gets old, no matter how many times we go back to the same story. Sometimes we need to go back to the familiar in the Bible to mull it over and let its message immerse us. I don't know about you, but I have a much easier time encouraging others to believe God's promises than I do believing them myself. Whether this is the seventh or the seventy-seventh time you've read this story, let's do a review. Hang with me and see if the Holy Spirit drops another piece of truth that will make this fresh for you and me.

The opening of the Book of Joshua is a narrative of passing a new mantle of leadership from Moses to Joshua. The torch has officially been handed down. If you remember, Moses's disobedience led God to prevent him from entering the Promised Land. While he was able to see it from a distance, he could not step foot into it. This is now Joshua's charge and territory.

To take their first steps into the Promised Land, the Israelites had to cross the Jordan River. It was the first major obstacle they had to face under new leadership. They were camping on the other side of the river, and Joshua sent two spies ahead to check out the land. They wanted to see what they were up against after they crossed the Jordan River, especially the city of Jericho, as it was a double-walled impregnable fortress.

So here we find the Israelites in chapters three and four as they prepare to cross the Jordan and take their first major city. The Jordan River was at its highest point in the season with its banks overflowing. It was nearly as much of a feat as the Red Sea the previous generation crossed forty years earlier. Joshua gives this instruction to the priests, "'Take up the ark of the covenant and pass on before the people.' So they took up the ark of the covenant and went before the people" (Joshua 3:6). The priests and leaders were then told to step out and put their sandaled feet into the raging Jordan River.

> And as soon as those bearing the ark had come as far as the Jordan, and the feet of the priests bearing the ark were dipped in the brink of the water (now the Jordan overflows all its banks throughout the time of harvest), the waters coming down from above stood and rose up in a heap very far away . . . And the people passed over opposite Jericho. Now the priests bearing the ark of the covenant of the LORD stood firmly on dry ground in the midst of the Jordan, and all Israel was passing over on dry ground until all the nation finished passing over the Jordan.
>
> —vv. 15–18

Can you even imagine? God first sent the leaders into the water, toward the flooded banks. The waters didn't part before they stepped in, and the ground didn't suck up all the water and leave a beautiful path signaling they could cross. No, they had to exercise faith and step into the deep water, trusting God would make way for them to cross over. That is God's way. He asks us to lead in faith when we are in a storm. He asks us to believe as the priests did as they were carrying the very embodiment of God's presence with them right to the middle of the river. God not only asks us to lead others in faith but in doing so, He asks us to lead ourselves in faith.

The priests didn't have time to debate the situation with Joshua. They didn't assess the height of the water or the speed of the rapids. They were called and knew they had to lead the way. It was their identity in the nation of Israel; they were Levites born into their sacred calling. They were appointed by God to lead the people with His presence symbolically displayed as they carried the Ark of the Covenant. They stood in the middle of the river until every last person, goat, sheep, and cart of household goods passed through to the other side. They not only had to lead the way but they had to sustain courage to stand firm footed, believing the waters wouldn't come and drown them. Were they scared? I bet they had doubts. As their feet planted toward the center of the river, the doubts didn't have a chance to take root because they had to cross the river on that day. Everything they knew about God was put to the test, and in some ways, they built a new way of thinking as they took their first steps.

When we are in a floodwater storm like the Israelites, we don't have time to debate the situation. We are summoned to lead with courage and strength. We pull up our bootstraps of faith and step out believing God knows what He is doing and that He will provide some dry ground, even when we see the rushing waters swirling around us.

One of the greatest floods in the history of the US was in 1927 when the Mississippi River's capacity was swollen past the point of no return. The flood impacted ten states. In New Orleans alone on April 15, 1927, fifteen inches of rain fell in eighteen hours, and four feet of water covered the city. The area was in ruins. There was no time to think; people just had to move to save themselves and get their families to higher ground.

When we are in a flood crisis in our lives, our faith works as the catalyst to move us to higher ground. God helps us put one foot in front of the other to keep from being overcome by the rushing waters. We can't wait; our faith pushes us to move forward. As God calls us to lead, we must activate our faith. Everything we believe stands on the foundation of our faith and keeps us from drowning in the floodwaters. I learn something new about my faith with every floodwater that comes and tries to submerge me.

Build a New Way of Thinking

One of the most crucial ways to stand strong in a storm capturing our faith is to create a new way of thinking when the floodwaters seek to paralyze us. Like Jenna did in the NICU unit on her terrible day. She exercised her faith and even spoke it out loud because she had to make a choice to confess that God was a good God and she could trust Him.

When we are overwhelmed with life and the stress starts to build, our natural response can often be to panic and let our negative thoughts overwhelm us. We start having thoughts of the dreaded what ifs.

What if I can't?

What if I won't make it?

What if it is a disaster?

We see the water overflowing on the banks. We focus on the rapids in the river. We hear the roar of the river upstream and wonder how long it will take to flood the valley. We look at our resources and realize we come up short. Our thoughts turn into fear, and all of this leads us away from seeing the presence of God standing firm-footed in the center of the riverbed, calling us to follow Him into the deep and lead us to higher ground.

Building a new way of thinking doesn't happen overnight. It takes a disciplined approach to conquering our negative thoughts when we feel overwhelmed. A few years back I realized I had gotten myself into a toxic thinking rut. No matter what I did to try and let go of the toxic thoughts I still struggled. I read my Bible, prayed, and asked God to deliver me from my toxic thinking and my inability to trust Him. If I was going to overcome, I knew I needed help. I learned from counselor Dr. Caroline Leaf in her book, *Who Switched Off My Brain?* "A healthy thought and toxic thought can both be built with mental rehearsal. But we can tear toxic strongholds down by choosing to bring the thought into conscious awareness for analysis, and then changing it through repentance and forgiveness (causing protein synthesis) and replacing it with the correct information, using Philippians 4:8 or something similar as a guideline."

I am an overachiever, overworker, overperfectionist, and overthinker. These dysfunctions in my life have come as a result of analyzing too much and not taking my thoughts and filtering them through God's Word and direction. I've had to work hard to retrain my brain so when I am in a storm, I can make a choice to confess my faith in a way that leverages my ability to see God and rise above my circumstances. It has been a long, arduous journey, but to date, my faith is rooted deeper. I live in Psalm 1:2–3, "His delight is in the law of the LORD, and on his law he meditates day and night. He is like a tree planted by streams of water that yields its fruit in its season, and its leaf does not wither. In all that he does, he prospers." My prayer is that I will be planted deep in Jesus by the river so when the floodwaters rise I will not only survive, but I will flourish and thrive.

The more I practice detoxing my thinking and focusing on God's Word the more I can rise above the obstacles. I move from being paralyzed, stuck on the riverbank watching the hopelessness of a rushing river, to a place of confident faith.

I have come to understand a few things about my thoughts.

First, my thoughts are real, and they are a result of what I observe, feel, and experience. I can't dismiss them and simply wish them away. I must deal with recurring negative thoughts or they will deal with me. I need to, as Dr. Leaf says, "replace it with the correct information." Taking the random thought and vetting it through Philippians 4:8 is a good place to start.

> Finally, brothers, whatever is true, whatever is honorable, whatever is just, whatever is pure, whatever is lovely, whatever is commendable, if there is any excellence, if there is anything worthy of praise, think about these things.

And we can't forget verse nine, "What you have learned and received and heard and seen in me—practice these things, and the God of peace will be with you." Want peace from toxic thoughts? Vet them through God's Word.

I have to make a choice to either accept or reject my thoughts. There is no other option. I will either cast a thought off or receive it. Some of the most helpful words of encouragement have come to me through Steven Furtick's book, *Crash the Chatterbox*. Furtick talks about training our minds to know the difference between the enemy's threats and God's whispers,

> The Enemy's threats are embedded in lies.
> God's whispers are rooted in truth.
> The Enemy's threats are designed to paralyze.
> God's whispers are empowered to mobilize.
> The Enemy's threats condemn vaguely.
> God's whispers instruct specifically.
> The Enemy's threats conspire to diminish hope.
> God's whispers empower change.
> The Enemy's threats are aimed to take you out.
> God's whispers speak a better Word to keep you in and move you forward.

Learning to discern in a time of crisis in a storm is critical to being able to stand strong. Furtick also suggests to play out the what ifs in our lives. Don't let the fear paralyze you at the moment. Play out what you see, feel, and experience. Ask yourself, if that happens, then what? Finish the sentences as the author encourages, "What if . . . That would . . . God will . . . "

Continue playing out all the what ifs you think might happen until you get to the promise of what you know God will do if your fear comes to pass. I can't tell you how that simple exercise has helped me move from feeding the lies and fears of my thoughts to moving me to rise and have the courage to weather the storm. And with Jesus I don't have to just weather the storm, I can stand firm and strong in knowing the One who is in control of the storm.

Rise Up

There is strength when we activate our faith by the way we think. What God gives us in the moments, I can't explain, but it is nothing short of a miracle. As we build up our faith by taking control of our thoughts, we can rise and lead by faith. There is a sense within us that calls out and says, I might be knee-deep in floodwaters, but with my God, I can do this.

It's the same cry of David when he was about to sling a stone into Goliath's forehead.

The same resolve as Esther when she boldly walked into the throne room and pled on her people's behalf to the king.

It is the same shout of confidence as Gideon when he ran with his shrunken army to overcome the Midianites.

It is the same strength as Deborah when she led her army against the oppressors of Israel.

It is the same passion that Peter had as he stood up to preach his first sermon at Pentecost.

God infuses us with His strength as we trust Him for every moment and especially as he delivers a tenfold dose when we need it most.

While this book is primarily geared toward leaders, some of you reading this book may not think of yourself so much as a leader but as someone who is temporarily filling a gap. You may have thought you needed a little encouragement right now. Or maybe you are a reluctant leader, hemming and hawing about what God is gently prodding you to do.

God is calling you to rise above the floodwaters because your kind of leadership is needed right now. I urge you not to ignore it. If your heart is beating fast as you are reading this sentence, then pay attention! I don't have to tell you throughout history God has called the most unlikely people to accomplish his purposes. He changed their thinking as he built up their faith and called them to be on mission. Where human eyes see someone incapable, God sees a leader. God's eyesight is different from ours. God doesn't have leadership myopia. His vision is crystal clear. And it might very well be that He has chosen you, right now. Don't hang back on the riverbank waiting for someone else to lead the way. Take a step of faith. Head straight toward the raging river and know that when you are stepping out in faith and confidence in God's calling, He will affirm everything you are to do at the moment. We don't live in the era of the Israelites where we have to physically carry the symbolic Ark of the Covenant to witness God's presence; we have God's presence because of the work of the Cross. We have the Holy Spirit who empowers us to do what we can't even imagine we could do without Him.

Trust

Faith like Jenna and Koby's doesn't get built up in the storm; it comes as a result of the storm. Jenna and Koby had to change their thinking. They stopped looking around at all the obstacles and activated their faith so they could rise no matter what happened to their sweet Judah.

As they cared for their other three children and continued to serve as they watched, waited, and prayed, they quietly trusted and believed. As the floodwaters are still rising, they are determined to believe even when it seems impossible. They have no choice but to trust. What else can they do? The still don't know the long-term effects of Judah's current condition—what the impact will be for the future of his brain, hearing, and vision. But they do know who God is, and His presence is palpable in this storm.

Jenna says:

> The hardest part when all settles down after a rough moment . . . is trusting again. It's a choice, friends. I actually slept last night (though it was here at the Ronald McDonald Family room!) because I chose to trust God again. He is trustworthy—we just need to make the choice again and again. My boy is here today, and I feel more thankful than ever—we hit the one-month mark later tonight. Sheesh—how great is God? Today I choose to trust again, as [Judah] will have his follow-up brain scan. Trust. Again.

Faith is trusting God knows what He is doing when the floods overwhelm us. He will provide whatever we need, which means He may recede the waters all the way or just partially. He may put us in a boat, or He may ask us to wade through the water holding onto Him as a life jacket. But I can assure you He will never leave us to drown or be so overcome we won't recover. He promises to make way for us to thrive in the midst of the flood. Standing strong in a storm creates an opportunity to rebuild our thinking, rise, and trust Jesus that on the other side of the river is God's promise for our future.

What toxic thinking do you need to get rid of? List those thoughts.

What is God calling you to claim in faith at this moment? What are you trying to overcome alone in the flood? Renounce it and hand it over to Jesus, inviting Him to be your life jacket as you wade in the floodwater.

Chapter Twelve

SNOWSTORM TEMPTATIONS

Moses: Learning to Delegate

> If you want to do a few small things right, do them
> yourself. If you want to do great things and make a
> big impact, learn to delegate.
>
> —John C. Maxwell, *Developing*
> *the Leaders Around You*

I had packed my computer back in my laptop bag and
was about to put my shoes on when I heard, in the security area, that our flight was cancelled. My husband and
I looked at each other in disbelief and wondered how we
were going to get to his mother's memorial from the small
airport near our home.

It was the latest in a series of weather-related incidents
in our lives. The northwest corner of the United States was
experiencing some brutal winter weather. I hadn't seen
that much snow since I was a kid. Just a few days before,
our son Jason and his wife Brittany, along with our sweet
little granddaughter, had been driving on an icy road and
couldn't stop. They hit another car. They were shaken but
not seriously injured. Shortly after, we received one of those
calls in the early morning hours you don't want to accept.
My husband's mother had died. Although we knew she
was ill and had been given warning, when we heard the
words, "She is gone," our hearts lurched in sadness.

Now we were traveling to California, and when our flight was cancelled, no other flights were available from our small airport. The only other option was to drive to Seattle and try to find another flight. The roads were still dangerous as we slowly made our way to the airport. I navigated the Internet on my phone to book another flight. There was one flight we possibly could make but the chances were doubtful in that weather. We decided to give it a try.

We drove nonstop for three hours and made it to the terminal with five minutes to spare. When we arrived at the gate, we saw the words we didn't want to see: flight delayed. Our hearts sank. Soon computers and servers started going down so no one could board any flight in the terminal. This lead to even more delays. After more calls, we finally were booked on a flight to San Diego. It wasn't the original plan, but it put us close enough to reach our destination.

Grateful but exhausted, we arrived in San Diego just before midnight. We picked up a car and landed on the doorstep of a friend who provided hugs and comfy beds after a "Can we stay with you?" text message from the airport in Seattle.

The next day we arrived a half-hour before the memorial service and were able to celebrate the life of our mom and spend time with our family. It was a journey of mishaps, and it was overwhelming when the situation was piling up. It's a good thing we have a sense of humor because at the height of the frustration we realized it was becoming so crazy it was laughable.

When snowstorms hit, a domino effect happens. Severe storms cause power outages due to heavy freezing rains. Roads are closed. Accidents litter the highways when you realize your everyday car is skating on the asphalt. Mounds of snow block driveways and cause schools to close. People can't get to work. The shelves empty at the grocery store. Children love it; adults hate it.

As leaders we bear the weight of feeling overwhelmed when a series of events acts like an out of control snowstorm creating hazardous conditions. It's easy to feel overwhelmed when a series of events creates a snowball effect that can run fast and furious. Before we know it, we are buried under what might feel like an avalanche.

Moses found himself like a downhill snowball gaining speed. Leading the Israelites in the desert wasn't for the faint of heart. There were the problems of what they were going to eat and where they would find water and shelter. Not to mention they had to fight enemies from time to time while they were trying to reach the Promised Land. He was the one responsible and had only his brother Aaron to help lead more than one million people. The Israelites had lived in a pagan nation for more than 400 years, and they had lost their understanding of who God was and how they were to follow Him. So God instructed Moses for each task and provided food and water as they traveled. He also led them with His presence—a pillar of cloud during the day and a pillar of fire by night. They had the most sophisticated GPS possible—God Himself—to guide them. And yet, they still encountered enormous problems.

Think about it with me for a moment. When God delivered the Israelites from Egypt, they had been living as slaves. They were at the bottom of the food chain of the Egyptian social structure. They had no rights, no opportunities, and no way to move up the ladder. Suddenly, they are completely free, but they were accustomed to living as slaves. They didn't understand how to live in freedom. Slavery meant they were told when to work, when to eat, and when to sleep. And while they couldn't own property, everything the slaves needed—food and shelter—was provided for them.

Suddenly, the Israelites are thrust into a life of freedom they hadn't experienced. They didn't quite know how to govern themselves or manage their affairs. In Exodus 16:2–3 we find the Hebrews grumbling and accusing Moses and Aaron of bringing them out to the desert to die. They had the gall to say, "Would that we had died by the hand of the LORD in the land of Egypt, when we sat by the meat pots and ate bread to the full, for you have brought us out into this wilderness to kill this whole assembly with hunger" (v. 3). And in Exodus 17:3 we find them complaining again, "Why did you bring us up out of Egypt, to kill us and our children and our livestock with thirst?"

Can you believe their response after all God did to rescue them? Before we are too quick to judge and condemn them for complaining, we have to try and understand their plight. I've never lived as a slave, and I doubt you have either. They couldn't read or write and certainly hadn't been free to run their lives. They didn't get to choose where to live. They didn't have an opportunity to be educated or excel in a career of their choice. Their masters planned every step and every moment of their lives from birth. That is what slavery is—no rights or freedoms. You were born a slave and you die a slave—all by the hand of your master.

It makes sense that Moses, who grew up in luxury in the house of the Pharaoh in Egypt, would find the Hebrews exasperating from time to time. When I think about all Moses had to face as a leader, I can see the snowball effect growing as I read chapter after chapter and empathize with his frustrations on how to help tame an unruly company of people. Moses was a reluctant leader responding to God's call when God spoke to him from a burning bush. He more than likely had been licking his wounds after escaping Egypt only to be herding sheep in the desert—a far contrast from living life as a prince as the son of the daughter of Pharaoh. He now found himself the leader of a nation of people that had no idea what they were getting themselves into when they left. They were discontent and idolized the comforts of slavery back in Egypt. They knew no different, and Moses's task was to try and guide them with God's help.

In Exodus 18, Moses's father-in-law pays a visit, reuniting Moses with his wife and children. Jethro marveled at the reports he heard of how God had delivered the people and performed miracles. Jethro observed Moses in the following days and how he was leading the people, attending to their needs and solving their problems. It was evident Moses was overwhelmed, sitting day after day, educating the people of God's laws and requirements, along with settling disputes amongst them. The truth is, the responsibilities were piling up. When Jethro saw this, he said:

> "What is this you are doing for the people? Why do you sit alone, and all the people stand around you from morning till evening?" And Moses said to his father-in-law, "Because the people come to me to inquire of God; when they have a dispute, they come to me and I decide between one person and another, and I make them know the statutes of God and his laws." Moses' father-in-law said to him, "What you are doing is not good. You and the people with you will certainly wear yourselves out, for the thing is too heavy for you. You are not able to do it alone. Now obey my voice; I will give you advice, and God be with you!"
>
> —Exodus 18:14–19

Jethro went on to detail a plan of delegation to lessen Moses's load and unburden him from feeling so overwhelmed and more importantly from burning himself out.

Jethro said to him, "That will make your load lighter, because they will share it with you. If you do this and God so commands, you will be able to stand the strain, and all these people will go home satisfied" (vv. 22–23 NIV).

Moses heeded his father-in-law's voice, and the load was lighter. Moses avoided the temptation to continue to try and handle it all by himself by listening to his wise father-in-law.

Jessica Jackley is best known for cofounding Kiva and later ProFounder, two organizations that help individuals loan small amounts of money, called microloans, to entrepreneurs throughout the world. She was caught in a snowball moment when she found out she was pregnant in 2011 and one of her investors declared she could quickly fail her company being in her situation. Despite her investor's disparaging words, the success of the business at the time was amazing because of Jessica's ability to delegate. She made a plan. Imagine that! Jessica pulled in and around her a strong team that could carry on in moments without her. She had a cofounder who shared the load with her. And you know what? She kept moving forward not because she was burning the midnight oil but because she knows how to delegate. A quote from her in an article in *Forbes* says it all, "As all entrepreneurs know, you live and die by your ability to prioritize. You must focus on the most important, mission-critical tasks each day and night, and then share, delegate, delay or skip the rest."

This is what Moses was up against as a leader—the need to dismantle the burden by delegating. And we as leaders are up against the very same problems. We can only lead our organization or church as far as we can successfully delegate. We can't do it all by ourselves, and God doesn't ask us to. He doesn't ask us to stop the snowball effect by ourselves because the truth is we can't. We will be crushed or worse—taken out.

Not delegating is a slippery slope to developing leadership martyr complex. And the moment we contract leadership martyr complex—pride in how much we are carrying in the name of Jesus—is the moment we forget serving is about God and not us. Don't be tempted by this snowball. There is something eerily satisfying in the basest sinful part of the soul to desire to extract all the credit without sharing the load. It is in a word—*narcissistic*—thinking and believing everything that happens is an extension of us, instead of an extension of God.

God is clear about sharing His glory reflects the focus back on God and not ourselves. Yes, that means delegating. No one person is a complete leader in and of himself or herself. In a *Harvard Business Review* article entitled, "In Praise of the Incomplete Leader," the authors assert, "It's time to end the myth of the complete leader: the flawless person at the top who's got it all figured out. . . . Only when leaders come to see themselves as incomplete—as having both strengths and weaknesses—will they be able to make up for their missing skills by relying on others."

Do you want to know a sure-fire way to stand strong in a storm? To have the confidence you won't be buried alive in the avalanche of your situation? Learn to ask for help. Yes, it's that simple. See your weakness for what it is— an opportunity to pull in and around you the strengths of your team so together you can weather the storm. Will you get a little frostbite from the cold and have to shovel piles of obstacles out of the way so you can see a clear path? Sure you will, but to thrive in the midst of the storm, you will have to learn how to effectively delegate. And that means to sit on your pride and realize you can't do it all by yourself. If you don't know how to delegate, find someone who does it masterfully and interview him or her. Get all their secrets and ask them to help you sift and structure to get through the issues.

Former US Secretary of State Donald Rumsfeld gives the perfect visual of what it means to delegate: "Don't be a bottleneck. If the matter is not a decision for the president or you, delegate it. Force responsibility down and out. Find problem areas, structure, and delegate. The pressure is to do the reverse. Resist it."

The snowball effect is a temptation to try and save the world all by yourself. Don't fall for it. Even Jesus delegated. The only thing Jesus did alone was going to the Cross. And the only reason He could do that was because He was the perfect Son of God and that was the plan. He is the only one that was called to save the world. Not you and not me, but Jesus.

Follow what Moses did and listen to the advice of those closest to you. Weigh in their thoughts and ponder them. I am sure when Moses saw his family for the first time after sending them away, he was not expecting to get counsel from his father-in-law. Jethro might have been the least likely candidate to give Moses advice. His father-in-law brought him more than his family; he brought him the life-saving information of how to stand strong in a storm. Delegate. It's the only way possible to move forward.

Where is your snowball effect right now?

What do you need to delegate immediately?

Who can you ask for help?

Chapter Thirteen
WORRY WINDS

Elijah: The Pitfall of Fatigue

> Worry does not empty tomorrow of its sorrow. It empties today of its strength.
>
> —Corrie ten Boom

Storms can knock the stuffing out of us. Look at Elijah and the storm he faced on Mount Carmel. He came to the end of himself after his great victory in 1 Kings 18 when the prophets of Baal were defeated. After that event he found himself running for his life from Queen Jezebel. She was determined to have his head after he killed all of her idolatrous prophets.

After running for his life, Elijah sat under a tree, ready to die. His exhaustion caused him to forget the faithfulness of God. He was cranky, tired, and hungry and he worried about Jezebel coming to get him. So God sent an angel with some food to restore him. The state of his soul was in disrepair, and he needed to sleep, eat, and get some perspective so he could start trusting God again and stop worrying. I've always wondered why he left his servant behind in Beersheba and traveled into the desert all by himself, "But he himself went a day's journey into the wilderness and came and sat down under a broom tree. And he asked that he might die, saying, 'It is enough; now, O LORD, take away my life, for I am no better than my fathers'" (1 Kings 19:4).

Elijah was just plain tuckered out and wanted to be all by himself. Maybe that's why he left his servant. He wanted to be miserable all alone. He had been working day and night for God, and all the emotional energy he gave at Mount Carmel defeating the prophets of Baal did him in. The words of Queen Jezebel elicited fear and doubt, and he decided to tell God he had enough. You notice the Lord didn't respond to his lament and request to end his life. Instead, God sent him something to eat to strengthen him. Not once but twice in between Elijah's naps. When the storm takes more than we bargain for, God knows what we need.

He doesn't beat us up and whip us to get back out and serve. "He knows how weak we are; he remembers we are only dust" (Psalm 103:14 NLT).

Sometimes what we need to dispel the winds of worry and gain a fresh perspective in our lives is to do as Elijah did. Take a nap. Eat something. In other words, take care of ourselves. God probably chose not to answer Elijah because He knew he was at the end of his reserves, and no amount of convincing would stop his whining until he got some rest.

Kevin and I had three of our grandchildren stay with us for twelve days last year. We called it Camp Cavanaugh. The youngest was nearly three and still needed naps. On the final day before their parents came home, I took them out on a rainy day on a field trip to the local museum. They had a great time, and we went to the bakery afterward to have lunch and a treat. On the way home, we made a quick stop at the grocery store. I knew I was pushing the envelope because the youngest needed her nap, but I wanted to grab a few things I forgot for dinner. She decided she didn't want to wear her coat out of the grocery store even though it was pouring rain. I knew if I gave in she would be whining about being wet when we got to the car, so I insisted. She had enough, and she let me know as I struggled to keep her coat on. It was like wrestling a snapping alligator to get her into the car seat. Nothing made her happy, and the waterworks ensued with shrieks and sobs. Her older brothers covered their ears and kept trying to reason with her to behave, but she would have none of it. She was done, she was finished, and she had enough. Exhausted after crying for about five minutes with snot and tears sticking to her face, she fell asleep on the drive home. I slipped her into bed once we got in the house. At dinner when her parents arrived, she said cheerfully from her seat, "Grandma, you are the best grandma ever!"

Just like my granddaughter, we need to remember that life looks different when we are recharged and rested. This holds true especially when we are battling the wind and waves in a storm. We have to recognize when we are at the end and pay attention to our warning signs of being completely done. When Kevin and I were in the darkest part of our storm, the one statement my counselor and those I was accountable to asked me over and over again, "What was I doing to take care of myself?" I was so caught up in trying to withstand the battering waves that I would forget what taking care of myself even looked like because I was so emotionally exhausted.

Ruth Haley Barton is founder and president of the Transforming Center, an organization that seeks to strengthen the souls of pastors, Christian leaders, and the organizations they serve. Ruth speaks of the exhaustion that plagues many leaders in her book, *Strengthening the Soul of Your Leadership*: "Everywhere I travel these days, those who are involved in church work and parachurch ministry report that they are exhausted in ministry and have despaired of finding a way of life that works. Many, in their more honest moments, dream of leaving ministry altogether, having come to the conclusion that this is the only way out of an unworkable lifestyle."

If we are to make it through a terrible storm and stand firm, we have to pay attention to the need to adopt a rhythm of rest and work.

I don't think it has to be all that complicated. We can use this story of Elijah as a basis for creating a checklist of what we should do when we find ourselves on the edge of having a meltdown and being done.

1. Don't leave your friends behind.

    Though we don't know the reason Elijah left his servant behind, it's never a good idea to isolate ourselves when we are in a storm. Find at least one trusted friend who will walk with you in your struggle.

2. Don't take yourself so seriously when you are empty.

    When you are tired and have pushed yourself past the point of no return, you can't take yourself too seriously. Your emotions can run away, causing you to worry, fear, and have a pity party. Bundle it up, speak it out, and then let it go. Like Elijah who whined to God in his moment of exhaustion, your feelings don't give you the accurate picture of what's happening when you are so exhausted.

3. Take a nap!

    Yes, you heard me. When we are sleep deprived nothing works well. We have to make space in our lives for our bodies and our minds to restore. Once Elijah had his pity party with God, "He lay down and slept under a broom tree" (1 Kings 19:5).

4. Nourish yourself.

    When I am stressed out to the max—I know this will sound weird—I forget to eat. When I remember, or my stomach reminds me, I don't always choose the best foods. I am working on it even as I am walking through some stressful days the past month. Elijah received heavenly food—cake and some water that an angel hand delivered to him.

Seems fairly basic, doesn't it? Sometimes we make the idea of recharging too complicated. We think we have to run to another country, sit on a beach, and do nothing for two weeks. Yes, that might be a good plan, but if we take care of ourselves by making healthy choices along the way, we have a much better chance of sustaining for the long haul. I am not trying to be too simplistic here, but I believe much of our exhaustion in leadership could be thwarted if we paid more attention to our soul and what it is saying to us. Our physical bodies and our emotional and mental states are all connected, and we would be wise to listen.

When the Wesleyan bands (an earlier version of modern discipleship small groups) of Christ followers got together, they would ask this particular question, "How is it with your soul?" Ruth Haley Barton addresses this in her book, *Strengthening the Soul of Your Leadership*, and challenges, "The soulful leader pays attention to such inner realities and the questions that they raise rather than ignoring them and continuing the charade or judging himself or herself harshly and thus cutting off the possibility of deeper awareness. Spiritual leadership emerges from our willingness to stay involved with our soul—that place where God's Spirit is at work stirring up our deepest questions and longings to draw us deeper into relationship with him."

When you and I find ourselves in a storm, if we are doing anything significant for God, these moments push us to the depths of our character. What we discover in the places of our character tested by the storm is a new self-awareness connecting us in a greater intimate relationship with God. That is why we can't ignore what's going on inside when we find ourselves under a broom tree as Elijah did.

Once we have gone through the checklist when we are exhausted, we then can discover what the voice deep inside of us is trying to communicate and put ourselves in a better place.

Elijah winds up at Mount Horeb in a different state than he was in the wilderness. He is waiting for God when a great storm of wind, an earthquake, and a fire all take place. He hangs back in the cave although God is drawing him out so He can talk to him. Elijah had seen the greatest victory on Mount Carmel, and the emphasis was in a spectacular miracle. Here on Mount Horeb God drew Elijah in the "sound of a low whisper. And when Elijah heard it, he wrapped his face in his cloak and went out and stood at the entrance of the cave. And behold, there came a voice to him and said, 'What are you doing here, Elijah?'" (vv. 12–13).

Elijah's response to God was to complain about the apostasy of Israel and report how he was the only one left who was faithful. He was still lamenting to some degree, probably feeling alone. But God reassured him there were 7,000 others who had not given a knee to the idol Baal and sold their integrity to a false god (v. 18). The temptation for Elijah here was to believe he was alone. God gave him his next assignment and declared Elisha would take his place as the next prophet.

As Elijah pressed in, God revealed Himself to him. Even though Elijah was discouraged—maybe even to the point of despair—he waited for God to speak. He didn't leave the wilderness and jump into the next thing. He waited for God to tell him where he should go and what he should do.

Being depleted puts us in a vulnerable position, and it is critical to wait and make sure we are listening to God's voice and not our own. That is paying attention to our soul. When we give heed to the inner life, we put ourselves in a posture to receive from God. Thrusting ourselves back on the hamster wheel when we aren't fully recovered puts us at risk of further damage and long-term consequences.

Facing a storm isn't a cakewalk, and honestly, it isn't something any of us sign up for. But there is something wildly beautiful in the outcome of a storm. It is what it does deep inside to us. It changes us, transforms who we are, and strengthens the core of who God has called us to be. Practicing the simple basics of weathering the storm like Elijah puts us in a position to hear God even when we are fragile. These moments become defining markers, changing the course of the story He is writing for each of us. We become stronger. We lead better and wiser. And we learn to depend on God in ways we might not have before.

So don't worry when the winds blow and threaten your peace of mind in the storm. Let God lead you to rest, feed your soul, and whisper the next steps He wants you to follow.

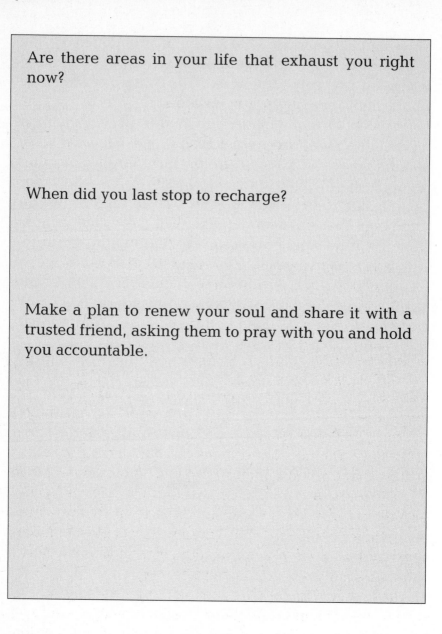

Are there areas in your life that exhaust you right now?

When did you last stop to recharge?

Make a plan to renew your soul and share it with a trusted friend, asking them to pray with you and hold you accountable.

Chapter Fourteen
TEMPEST TRIALS

Judas and Jesus: Betrayal

> It is easier to forgive an enemy than to forgive a friend.
>
> —William Blake

In the early years of our ministry Kevin and I attended a weeklong conference for pastors and ministry leaders. It was held at a beautiful hotel on the Columbia River on the border of Washington and Oregon. It became one of the highlights for us each year as we anticipated getting away to be refreshed and to learn from veteran speakers and teachers. We also had the opportunity to connect with other leaders and made some lasting friendships. It was our annual pilgrimage four hours from our home where we gathered with our tribe. These were people we understood and likewise who understood what it meant to serve as pastors and leaders in a church.

Throughout the week as we sat together sharing our stories, one common theme seemed to emerge—betrayal and brokenness. Each year as we attended the conference we realized how volatile we were serving in leadership. We listened, learned, and prayed so when the time came, we could at least be somewhat prepared. Because if you've been involved in any sort of ministry for very long, the word *betrayal* will arrive at your doorstep.

Imagine with me these scenarios. Without revealing names, places, or details, these are true stories I've heard from others or ones I've experienced myself.

- You've invested years together as ministry partners and are best friends. A misunderstanding happens, and your ministry partner begins slandering you behind your back to the team. A full-blown eruption happens that divides and creates confusion in the organization.

- Your close friend who has a difficult marriage begins to confess feelings for your spouse (a staff member/pastor), and an emotional affair ensues behind your back. Your spouse recognizes the danger and course corrects, but your friend blames your spouse and tries to pit you against your spouse.

- A power struggle happens on the board and a controlling board member comes against you and sabotages the facts of the situation to gain support.

- You are working with several organizations on a large-scale project that will reach across the nation. A flurry of misunderstanding happens over which organization will be the recognized leader. It isn't getting resolved because it centers on who is investing most of the time and finances. Some of the leaders decide to pull out after they had made a commitment to you and to the project.

- You work to try to set leadership standards and boundaries for your team. After repeated conversations and accommodation with a few of the team members, they become angry and without warning gather others to discredit your leadership.

These scenarios repeat themselves over and over again with different players and circumstances but nonetheless they happen far too often. The hardest thing, of course, is when a situation like one of these happens to you or me. It can knock the wind out of us, and we can flail momentarily as we try and find the anchor in the tempest of the storm.

When we have been deeply misunderstood, even betrayed, we have to be willing to commit to obey and forgive those who have misunderstood us and possibly even tried to discredit us in the process. But it is *so very* tough! It is probably one of the hardest things you or I will ever have to do.

In many ways, I feel like the least likely candidate to mentor anyone on the topic of forgiveness. It is a journey I have found myself on regularly. I've read countless articles, books, and workbooks on forgiveness. The concept and action of forgiveness has been a test of my faith. It has tested what I believe about God and relationships, and yet I still find myself on the other side of looking at forgiveness in ways I hadn't seen before.

I have considered myself a very forgiving person. I have tried to live by a value of not holding grudges and keeping short accounts, and for the most part, this practice has served me well.

I give myself 100 percent in relationships with others and love getting to the heart of the matter with friends and family. When relationships don't work, I sometimes try too hard, and it gets me in trouble. I take on more in the relationship than is healthy, which counselors call codependency. In other words, I take on the feeling of responsibility for other people's happiness. It is a family curse my sister and I laugh about sometimes as we try to disentangle ourselves from this unhealthy behavior.

But on occasion I am not that good at forgiving. You see, forgiveness is easier, and I say this cautiously, when things are resolved. It is much harder when there is no resolution on the horizon. When you try so desperately to be understood and there still is no resolution can be a difficult place to be when trying to forgive.

It has been said that forgiveness is a gift you give yourself. Why is that? Because when we forgive we set ourselves free from the opposite of forgiveness—bitterness, a poison that contaminates and changes us. Can I dare to forgive this person who betrayed me? Can I dare to let it go? Can I entrust the situation, the person, and the pain to God?

Choosing to forgive encompasses three simple truths—letting go, leaning in, and trading lies for love.

Letting Go

We can't forgive if we don't let go. Stop nursing, rehearsing, rehashing, and reliving the wounding and the hurt. Some of this is necessary for healing, but at some point, we need to learn to let go and let God handle it. I have to confess; I've let go and then taken it back over and over again. I've had to ask God to help me let go so I can let Him do the work both to my heart and the situation. It is so very difficult!

Anne Graham Lotz says in her book, *Wounded by God's People*, "I have come to a turning point where I want to be healed more than I want to be wounded." Wow! When I read that it was like an arrow piercing my soul. I had to come to a point where I could ask myself as Anne did, do I want to be healed more than I want to be wounded?

Our granddaughters love the Disney movie *Frozen*, which took the box office by storm in 2013. I see little girls everywhere that aspire to be like one of the main characters, Elsa and Anna. One of the theme songs of the movie, "Let It Go," is sung by Elsa as she comes face to face with her need to forgive herself for hurting her little sister and misusing her magical gift. It changed her life because she couldn't let go and forgive herself, and so her heart froze, which in turn froze the kingdom around her. She isolated to protect herself, but it only caused more pain and hurt.

When I go to that place of isolation, nobody wins, my heart grows cold, and it impacts everyone around me and reels you and me into a kingdom of isolation.

So the first step is to recognize I can only change me, not others.

I can't make people see what I want them to see, only God can.

I become frozen. So I have no other choice but to *let go* if I want to be vibrant and whole. The first step is to *let go* and *let God* do *His job*.

Leaning In

Part of leaning in is to name your hurt, your loss, and your betrayal, and don't ignore the pain. Get help. We aren't meant to do life alone. I've already said this several times in other chapters. If you are like me and have trouble letting go, ask yourself why. What will you lose if you let go? I found I was worried my forgiveness may still cause me to be misunderstood and rejected by the betrayal. Some of my fears did come true but God has helped me to face my fears head on in the midst of the storm.

Jesus died on a Cross for crimes he didn't commit. And as He hung on that Cross, He asked God to forgive us. He asked God to forgive mankind for betraying Him and killing Him. And as He said, "For they know not what they do" (Luke 23:34), He forgave. He let go even of what Judas did—betraying him with a kiss. Betrayed by a man he had spent loving, teaching, and being a part of the brotherhood for three years.

Jesus is our example, our hope, and our healing. He was wounded, and Isaiah says, "With his wounds we are healed (Isaiah 53:5). It truly is a mystery. It's supernatural and honestly a phenomenon. Somehow, as I call upon God to help me forgive, He imparts within me the power to forgive. It is a miracle because I can't do it by myself.

Have you seen the two Dutch grandmothers, An and Ria, on YouTube? They attempt to take a flight together for the first time. In their seventies, An and Ria dare to risk together, to have the courage to do something they hadn't done before. During and after the flight, they laugh, they cry, and they say they feel younger because they are free from their fears of flying.

That's exactly what happens when we engage the God of the Universe in helping us to forgive when it is painful, horrible, and awful. He sets us free. When we can't forgive we stay locked in the pain of our fear that justice somehow won't be served. We think God is turning His back on what happened and letting the other person off the hook. But you and I know better because of what His Word says: "Don't hit back; discover beauty in everyone. If you've got it in you, get along with everybody. Don't insist on getting even; that's not for you to do. 'I'll do the judging,' says God. 'I'll take care of it'" (Romans 12:17–19 *The Message*).

God will take care of it. He can be trusted.

When we choose to forgive, He empowers us, encourages us, helps us, and sets us free from the prison of unforgiveness and all its baggage.

Isaiah 50:10–11 (*The Message*) says this:

> Who out there fears GOD, actually listens to the voice of his servant? For anyone out there who doesn't know where you're going, anyone groping in the dark, here's what: Trust in GOD. Lean on your God! But if all you're after is making trouble, playing

with fire, go ahead and see where it gets you. Set your fires, stir people up, blow on the flames, but don't expect me to just stand there and watch. I'll hold your feet to those flames.

Trading Lies for Love

Martin Luther King Jr. helps us to press in the challenge further of letting go and leaning in with this quote, "We must develop and maintain the capacity to forgive. He who is devoid of the power to forgive is devoid of the power to love. There is some good in the worst of us and some evil in the best of us. When we discover this, we are less prone to hate our enemies."

You see, the lie I believed for a long time was if I waited for the situation to resolve I could forgive. And in the meantime what happened to my heart is it began to shrink. It got cold, and the talons of bitterness crept in. The old unhealthy pattern of codependency reared its ugly head, feeding me the line that I couldn't move on until there was resolve.

The wounds from my marriage crisis made me feel traumatized. My inability to truly forgive scared me to death. I knew I had to do something different. I could *let go, lean in*, refute my deception of unhealthy thinking, and learn to *love* in spite of the unresolved issues. It is a conscious choice of obedience to act and forgive.

So I traded the lie the enemy was whispering for love. I looked at the face of God who said to me in Psalm 34:18, "The LORD is near to the brokenhearted and saves the crushed in spirit."

You see, holding onto the lie wasn't going to help my faith to believe God still loved me and cared about my pain. But this is a promise I hold on to—God is not expecting me to flail my heart open to be trampled on and stepped on.

He asks us in Proverbs 4:23 to "Keep your heart with all vigilance, for from it flow the springs of life."

In every situation of our woundedness, betrayal, and hurt, there are appropriate measures to be taken. We need skillful companions along the journey, a good friend, a counselor, or a mentor, especially when we are in severe pain.

So what does walking in forgiveness mean? I can't answer for you, only for me. Only you can provide the answer, and it is between you and God and hopefully with the help of skilled counselors. I wouldn't dare prescribe a formula of what forgiveness looks like for reconciliation. Each situation is different. I do know one staunch truth: we are called to forgive. It is the greatest gift we can give ourselves and is a perfect opportunity to give grace to others. But the healing journey of reconciliation is a delicate process.

I have found myself over and over again asking, but what does this mean for me? It is complicated. I won't pretend it is easy. Sometimes we are asked to walk a hard road of forgiveness and reconciliation. But remember not to confuse forgiveness with trust and allow it to keep you from forgiving. God doesn't necessarily ask us to trust a person who has betrayed us. Forgiveness is a process. We are called to forgive, so our hearts remain pure and no weed of bitterness takes root.

Let's take a refresher course on what the Bible says about forgiveness.

Matthew 18:21–22: Peter asked how often one should forgive. Jesus said seventy times seven.
Luke 17:3–5: We can't forgive on our own, we need God's help.
Colossians 3:13: As the Lord has forgiven me, I must also forgive.

Matthew 6:14: If we don't forgive, God will not forgive us. Ouch!

Here are some things to remember about forgiveness adapted from thoughts from Rick Warren's teaching on the subject.

1. Forgiveness is not conditional. In other words, it's not based on someone else's response.
2. Forgiveness doesn't excuse behaviors or minimize the offense. Forgiveness prevents the other person's behavior from destroying your heart.
3. Forgiveness doesn't equal trust. Forgiveness is your part in the reconciliation. Trust must be rebuilt over time.
4. Forgiveness is not forgetting. Once you choose to forgive the person who hurt you, you can actually be sympathetic and begin to pray for them.
5. Forgiveness leads to healing and unlocks your heart. Forgiveness is a gift we give ourselves that allows us to move forward with our lives instead of being trapped in the past by bitterness and resentment.
6. I forgive. First, because I've been forgiven by God. Second, unforgiveness makes me miserable. And third, in the future I will need to be forgiven. The benefit of forgiveness is not for others but for ourselves.

There is a powerful principle of forgiveness in the story of Luke when Jesus has dinner at the home of a Pharisee. When a woman came in and began washing Jesus' feet, the Pharisee was surprised Jesus would let this woman touch him. The Pharisee knew her reputation. If Jesus was who He said He was, He would know her reputation too, and He certainly wouldn't have let this unclean woman touch Him. But Jesus knew this Pharisee's thoughts.

> Then he turned to the woman and said to Simon,
> "Look at this woman kneeling here. When I entered
> your home, you didn't offer me water to wash the
> dust from my feet, but she has washed them with her
> tears and wiped them with her hair. You didn't greet
> me with a kiss . . . she has not stopped kissing my
> feet. You neglected the courtesy of olive oil to anoint
> my head, but she has anointed my feet with rare per-
> fume. I tell you, her sins—and they are many—have
> been forgiven, so she has shown me much love. But
> a person who is forgiven little shows only little love."
>
> —Luke 7:44–47 NLT

Most of the time this passage is taught from the woman's
point of view and her sincerity of worship. And that's certainly a valid viewpoint. But God gave me new eyes to see
the heart of this story. It's not just about giving my all to
Jesus in worship as the woman did, but it is a story about
forgiveness and my willingness to love much because I've
been forgiven much.

If we don't choose to forgive, our influence will waver.
Our leadership will stagnate. We will lose our special
assignment of influence. The profound words of Jesus in
this story to the Pharisee who is judging the woman for her
act of worship is in what Jesus says, "But a person who is
forgiven little shows only little love." In other words, we
can't possibly love others with a full heart if we can't forgive
the ones that have hurt, betrayed, and misunderstood us.

If you have been in leadership long enough, you will
be betrayed and wounded. I am not telling you anything
you don't already know. We as leaders often think we are
exempt from betrayal, but it will come. We have to lead
the way in letting go, leaning in, and replacing the lies
we believe about forgiveness. Our followers are watching. Those we are mentoring are waiting to see if we will
react or respond.

God brought this truth home to me one afternoon. I was headed to the local café to have some lunch and had planned to do some journaling and reflecting. I noticed an elderly woman sitting in the next booth all by herself. I had an overwhelming urge to invite her to have lunch with me. It wouldn't go away. When God whispers, He is insistent. I argued with God about how this was my time; I didn't really want to talk to anybody. He wouldn't leave me alone, and so wanting to be obedient, I asked her if she wanted to join me for lunch. She gave a resounding, yes, and I cringed inwardly and thought, "OK God, this better be good!"

As we ate, she began to tell me her story. She had been in church all her life and been woefully betrayed. I empathized with her, but more and more bitterness of unforgiveness oozed like a poison. Her heart appeared tainted by her inability to forgive. God gave me a strong warning in my soul and whispered to me that if I couldn't let go, lean in, and trust Him with forgiving, I too would end up like this woman.

This realization scared me to death. It was like looking into my future thirty years down the road. I left that day shaken by what God showed me. I told God I needed his help to fully work through forgiving those who had wounded me. It was a defining moment, and whenever I am tempted to hold on to the pain of unforgiveness, I remember that day at my local café.

How about you? What do you need to let go of and let God handle? Who do you need to release in surrender to the one who promises He will take care of it? Do it now while the conviction is hovering over your heart. Don't let the temptation of the tempest of unforgiveness steal your future.

Where do you need to let go?

Where do you need to lean in?

Spend some time journaling your thoughts. Take a chance to have a conversation with God about it and lean in to listen to what He might be saying about your situation.

Chapter Fifteen
THE GATHERING STORM

King Jehoshaphat:
Leading into the Future

When you can't trace His hand you can trust His heart.

—Charles Spurgeon

I grew up reading stories about missionaries and others who were imprisoned for their faith. And I listened first-hand to the faith stories of my grandparents who lived under Communist Russia at the turn of the twentieth century. As young children, they lost siblings, family members, and farms to the ravages of communism.

I leaned in and listened when my grandmother shared about the time her family was starving, and she cried out to God. He brought her attention to the singing birds in the meadow. God reminded her of Matthew 6:26, "Look at the birds of the air; they neither sow nor reap or gather into barns, and yet your heavenly Father feeds them. Are you not of much more value than they?" He whispered to her heart He would take care of her family like He takes care of the birds. She felt led to follow the singing of the birds into the meadow where she discovered a berry bush. She was able to stave off the hunger for a few more hours for her family.

I sat with eyes wide as my grandfather shared stories of dodging bullets and capture to secure freedom so he and my grandmother could have passage to come to the United States. My mother's family had been homeless for 27 years, living before, during, and after the war in places God provided, including a refugee camp and with a kind farmer who took the family in for seven years, five of them staying in one room.

Was there doubt? Probably, yes. Was there fear? Most likely. But what I heard intertwined in these stories was an unstoppable faith. The faithfulness of God taking care of my family as the winds of the storm blew over their lives. When they finally crossed into New York Harbor in 1950 with the Statue of Liberty welcoming their arrival, they had hope.

My heritage gives me the courage to stand strong in the storms that I know will be ahead. It is the truth of what my grandparents believed that helped them to persevere, and it is what I hold onto. It is my legacy anchor. I feel a great responsibility to develop that same kind of trust in the truth that has been passed down to me.

When the storm blows and the winds seek to overtake me, I remember my grandparents. I stand on the faith legacy they passed on to me, and I am comforted. Do I still worry? Doubt? Have trouble trusting? Yes, I do. Somehow the security of knowing they made it through those storms makes me feel brave and gives assurance that I will too.

The world seems to be unraveling before our eyes. Never have I seen so much division and unrest in my lifetime. If I focus on all the negative, I will worry about the winds of a storm that seek to blow me off the foundation I know to be true. I won't be able to trust in the truth God wants me to stand on.

We've talked about many types of storms in this book—from hurricanes to snowstorms. We aren't in control of any

of those storms, and the storm that is growing in our culture is picking up fast and furious. We as people of God
and the men and women who are in leadership have to
stand on what we know to be true so we can weather
what's ahead.

We don't have the privilege of scheduling our storms
or controlling the storms gathering in the distance. Will
they hit unexpectedly? Yes, storms will continue in our
lives intermittently, and with force. The enemy would love
nothing more than for the winds to destroy us and take us
out. We don't have to let him win; we can stand strong in
a storm with immovable influence.

I want to finish the book with one of my most cherished
stories in the Bible from 2 Chronicles 20. It illustrates the
truth of anchoring ourselves in God for the future. It is
the story of King Jehoshaphat when he was facing the
dreaded Moabites and Ammonites. His kingdom was
facing insurmountable odds. And yet, he didn't rely on his
own strength, he pressed into God so tightly, and he saw
God's deliverance.

I want to follow in Jehoshaphat's footsteps as this great
victory story tells us. God has pummeled this story into my
being over and over again. I mean pummeled in a positive way, not the negative picture we might get in our
minds of someone thrashing the tar out of another person.
God beat the principles of this story down into the core of
my soul. It helps me remember when I am up against the
storm of the century and all looks hopeless that God will
deliver me with a force greater than any Star Wars movie
could make us believe.

There are some concrete steps we can extract in this
account that can help you and me as we move into the
future. Because we know it is not a matter of *if* but *when*
we will face another storm.

Believe

King Jehoshaphat believed in God. He not only believed, but he genuinely believed, and this belief was evident by his commitment to follow God's commandments. He knew he was up against more than he could resolve on his own: "Then Jehoshaphat was afraid and set his face to seek the LORD, and proclaimed a fast throughout all Judah" (2 Chronicles 20:3). He didn't consult the false gods his father King Asa had followed, he obeyed the Lord and kept His commands because He believed in the one true God. He didn't give up and wasn't swayed by the greed of the idol worshipers in the land. His heart was devoted to the truth.

When the winds come, and they will come, when they decide to blow and blow hard, only the truth will keep us standing strong in the storm. The truth is what anchors our belief. When we follow the truth, the unquestionable truth of God's Word even when the winds threaten, we will be sustained. I know I am not telling you anything new, but when caught in a horrific storm, it is easy to forget God's faithfulness and what God has already built into your life and mine. God knows exactly how much of His truth is embedded in our hearts, and He will only challenge us to the point where we can fully trust Him. He knows we have doubts and uncertainties just like Jehoshaphat—he was afraid.

The most important thing you and I can do in a crisis is to believe the truth of who God is. The temptation is to abandon God and believe the lies that Satan would whisper.

See, God has forgotten about you.

He is busy with somebody else.

You can't trust Him.

Satan's strategy hasn't changed from the beginning of time. Don't fall for it.

Gather

Jehoshaphat gathered His people together (v. 4). Let's follow his example. Gather your friends and tell them what you are struggling with. Let them fast and pray with you for victory. Don't try to fight it alone. That is why God calls us to live together in community, and that includes leaders. Leadership can be lonely, and yet we have to find spaces in our lives to make room for real friends. Not just people we serve with and who we lead but authentic friendships who can stand with us when we are hurting.

Remember

After he called the people to pray and fast, King Jehoshaphat launched into a public conversation with God for everyone to hear. He reminded God of who He was by repeating back to God the annals of history, recounting the mighty faithfulness of God to Israel.

Do you think God needed to hear all that? Of course not; He knew every syllable of every word better than Jehoshaphat did. But when we cry out to God, it's OK to remind Him and to remember how He has been faithful to you in the past. What that does is provide a release to be able to fully trust in the truth of who God is in our life. There is something about speaking it out loud with witnesses present. King Jehoshaphat was rehearsing for himself and his people the faithfulness of God, not because God needed to be reminded but because they needed to remember. King Jehoshaphat ended his account with, "O our God, will you not execute judgment on them? For we are powerless against this great horde that is coming against us. We do not know what to do, but our eyes are on you" (v. 12).

There it is, the grand confession, and every one of us need to adopt this power-releasing phrase in our vocabulary. "We don't know what to do, but our eyes are on you." When we come to the end of ourselves and know there is no way we can muster up the strength and resources to fight the battle in the storm, I think God as a loving parent who smiles and says, "Now you understand who I am and what I can do."

Trust

Here is where the down and dirty steps take place. Jehoshaphat could see the storm in the distance. They might have heard the rumble of the hobnailed sandals of the soldiers marching and the noise of the chariots flying across the landscape. They knew the enemy was approaching.

And yet as panic rose in them, God gives specific actions through the prophet Jahaziel: "Listen, all Judah and inhabitants of Jerusalem and King Jehoshaphat. Thus says the LORD to you, 'Do not be afraid and do not be dismayed at this great horde, for the battle is not yours but God's. Tomorrow go down against them. Behold, they will come up by the ascent of Ziz. You will find them at the end of the valley, east of the wilderness of Jeruel. You will not need to fight in this battle. Stand firm, hold your position, and see the salvation of the LORD on your behalf, O Judah and Jerusalem.' Do not be afraid and do not be dismayed. Tomorrow go out against them, and the LORD will be with you" (vv. 15–17).

Can you follow the trail of encouragement here?

Do not be afraid or dismayed.
The battle is not yours but God's.
You will not need to fight in this battle.

Stand firm.
Hold your position.
See the salvation of the Lord on your behalf.
The Lord will be with you.

Can you see it? We don't have to battle alone when the storm gathers on the horizon. God promises to give us everything we need at the exact moment we need it. We can lead with confidence in our homes, in our churches, our workplaces, and communities. Let this be verses of reassurance for us in our vulnerable places.

Whatever storm clouds are gathering in the future, we can take courage in this story and know the God of Jehoshaphat is the same God of us, and He promises to be with us. He won't leave the scene of the action.

Praise

We can't forget the rest of the story. After they received the promises of deliverance, the king bowed down and worshipped. They probably worshipped in relief and in anticipation of what they would witness. "The Levites . . . stood up to praise the LORD, the God of Israel, with a very loud voice" (v. 19).

When is the last time you stood up in a storm and just worshipped at the top of your voice? The enemy hates our worship and our praise to God. He can't stand it. When we rip it out from the inmost places of our soul and sing until we can't sing anymore, God is fighting for us in the dark places of the heavenly. When discouragement seeks to overwhelm me, I have to worship. The darkness flees and reminds me of who is in control of my situation. So do it. Put on some worship music and crank it out. Sing until you can't sing another note and take the ground back the enemy is trying to steal from you. You will feel better, I promise. Don't let the gathering clouds rob you from trusting the only one who can sustain you and help you flourish in the midst of your storm.

The rest of the story is a beautiful picture of God's people trusting Him with everything they believe. King Jehoshaphat rises the next morning and addresses the crowd by telling them to "Believe in the LORD your God, and you will be established; believe his prophets, and you will succeed" (v. 20).

When they worshipped victory came, "As soon as they started shouting and praising, GOD set ambushes against the men of Ammon, Moab, and Mount Seir as they were attacking Judah, and they all ended up dead. The Ammonites and Moabites mistakenly attacked those from Mount Seir and massacred them. Then, further confused, they went at each other, and all ended up killed" (vv. 22–23 *The Message*).

God set the ambushes. He did what He does best—fights for us, stays with us, and carries us when we are overwhelmed.

There is a storm gathering on the horizon, and it seems like all at once the whole world is going mad. Let's commit to living like King Jehoshaphat, keeping an eye on the gathering storm. Let's live with the conviction of not knowing what to do but with eyes fixated on the God of the storm and the future.

Let's lead with immovable influence anchored and standing strong by believing Jude 24 (*The Message*):

> And now to him who can keep you on your feet, standing tall in his bright presence, fresh and celebrating—to our one God, our only Savior, through Jesus Christ, our Master, be glory, majesty, strength, and rule before all time, and now, and to the end of all time. Yes.

**If you enjoyed this book, will you consider
sharing the message with others?**

Let us know your thoughts at info@newhopepublishers.com. You
can also let the author know by visiting or sharing a photo of the
cover on our social media pages or leaving a review at a retailer's
site. All of it helps us get the message out!

Twitter.com/NewHopeBooks

Facebook.com/NewHopePublishers

Instagram.com/NewHopePublishers

———————

New Hope® Publishers is a division of Iron Stream Media,
which derives its name from Proverbs 27:17,
"As iron sharpens iron, so one person sharpens another."

This sharpening describes the process of discipleship,
one to another. With this in mind, Iron Stream Media provides
a variety of solutions for churches, missionaries, and nonprofits
ranging from in-depth Bible study curriculum and
Christian book publishing to custom publishing and consultative
services. Through the popular Life Bible Study and Student Life
Bible Study brands, ISM provides web-based full-year and
short-term Bible study teaching plans as well as printed
devotionals, Bibles, and discipleship curriculum.

For more information on ISM and New Hope Publishers,
please visit

IronStreamMedia.com

NewHopePublishers.com

OTHER NEW HOPE
LEADERSHIP RESOURCES

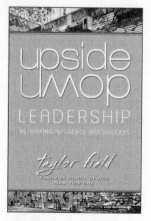

ISBN: 978-1-59669-342-5
N124247
$14.99

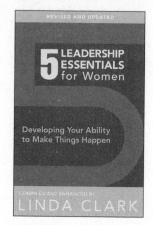

ISBN: 978-1-59669-431-6
N154110
$15.99

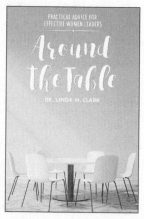

ISBN: 978-1-62591-529-0
N184103
$15.99

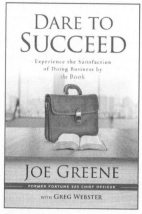

ISBN: 978-1-62591-527-6
N184101
$16.99

NEW HOPE®
P U B L I S H E R S

For more information, including where to purchase,
please visit **NewHopePublishers.com**.